CALL TO CONNECTION

BRINGING SACRED TRIBAL VALUES

INTO MODERN LIFE

CAROLE KAMMEN & JODI GOLD

Commune-A-Key Publishing

Salt Lake City, Utah

COMMUNE-A-KEY PUBLISHING
P.O. Box 58637
Salt Lake City, UT 84158
(801) 581-9191
(801) 581-9196 Fax

Kammen, Carole
Call to connection: bringing sacred tribal values into modern life /
by Carole Kammen & Jodi Gold.
p.   cm.
Includes bibliographical references and index.
ISBN: 1881394-20-4 (alk. paper)
1. Conduct of life. 2. Spiritual life. 3. Tribes—Miscellanea.
I. Gold, Jodi. II. Title.
BJ1595.K294 1998
170'.44—dc21   97-48969
CIP

$14.95 USA
$20.95 CANADA

Cover & Interior Design: Nita Ybarra Design, San Francisco, CA
Photography: Moya Photographx, Berkeley, CA

This book is designed as a tool to guide the reader to greater self-knowledge and connection to others. If the reader experiences undesirable results, consequences or behaviors, the authors and publisher are not to be held responsible. If your personal history suggests that you may need psychotherapeutic assistance, the authors recommend that you seek professional guidance before, during and after reading this book.

DEDICATION

To all those who seek

to live life

with an open heart,

and

to our partnership,

an enduring act of

grace and love.

ACKNOWLEDGMENTS

We didn't intend to write this book. It burst out of us one day while we sat on the floor of a little hotel room in Palm Springs. This book had a mind of its own. It intended to be birthed, and it would not be denied.

This book could not have been written without the Temenos Tribe. It exists because of them. For the past eleven years, individuals have sat in our circles, bringing with them their love, hope, vision, and dreams. It is their courage to open their hearts and share their life stories with one another that brought alive and made real the power of tribe. We deeply appreciate Lynnaea Lumbard for beginning and nourishing Temenos for so many years.

Even as we left Palm Springs, we didn't dare to imagine that we could be authors. We knew that this book needed to be written, so we set off to find someone to write it. Author Hal Bennett was the first person to believe in the book, and in us. With his help and encouragement we became writers, and with his skill as a magician and alchemist, our two voices became one.

Like any new parent, our lives and the lives of those around us became irrevocably changed. Our extraordinary staff: Tina Benson, Lily Myers, Tim Kelley, Bob Beban, Jan Cohn, Catherine Dolan-Haas, Patricia Johnson, Susan Graham-Fox, Karen Palmer, and Tambra Harck, shouldered the responsibility of the teaching and day to day running of our organization, graciously giving us the room to write. They were the sounding boards for our fears, and cheerleaders for our ideas. We could never thank them enough for their support, inspiration, and most of all for living and creating sacred tribe every day.

We could never express enough gratitude to Bruce McDiffett. He came through for us no matter what, and often when we were too uninitiated to know what we needed. He was unwavering in his editing of the manuscript, technical advice, and holding the vision with us. Bruce generously spent many sleepless nights in service to the book, and in support of us.

Many others pitched in with expertise, support, and generous enthusiasm to midwife this. Marcia Weider, Kathy Altman, Laurie Saltzman, and our publisher Caryn Summers helped us learn to navigate the world of publishing. Teri Augustine, Rachel Sater, and Debbie Heller brought tireless work and attention to detail.

And finally, we want to acknowledge Zachary, who brings so much love and meaning to our lives, and reminds us every day of simple joy.

CONTENTS

PART I: A CALL TO CONNECTION

PART II: THE SEVEN SACRED TRIBAL VALUES

PART III: PRACTICING THE VALUES IN MODERN LIFE

PART

I

A CALL TO CONNECTION

INTRODUCTION

One of the truths of our time is this hunger deep in people all over the planet for coming into relationship with each other.

—*Mary Caroline Richards*

A STORY OF TRIBE

A TWO-WEEK-OLD baby is handed to his grandfather, who stands in a circle with forty men of all ages. The grandfather is the oldest man there. He stands with his son next to him in the men's circle, knowing that his wife and the baby's mother are standing in the women's circle around them. The baby is passed around the circle. As the grandfather watches his grandson moving from one man to another, he listens to a man in the circle say, "This child is part of the promise, the hope."

The grandfather looks around, amazed that he didn't know any of these men seventy-two hours before. An old man now, he looks into the baby's face and sees the face of his own father, long dead. He looks into the face of the baby's father and remembers himself holding him as a baby thirty-two years before.

Until this moment, the grandfather hadn't realized how much his own living had taught him, how many lines had been etched upon his face by the experiences that have molded his character. He looks into the eyes of the younger men in the circle and recognizes himself as the old man he has become: the elder. He knows that it is time for him to rest, to slow down. He'd known that for a long time, but somehow he now recognizes what this means.

At the core of the circle is something ancient, even primordial, a sense of an identity beyond their separate, individual lives. Tears threaten, the men are overwhelmed, yet shy about expressing what they are feeling at this moment. Later, a few of them would talk about a bewildering feeling of longing, a longing that in this poignant moment was satisfied, filling a need for which they had no name. They had not known whether to celebrate what they were feeling, standing in this circle with other men—grandfathers, fathers, uncles, brothers, peers—or to grieve over the years they had gone without being able to draw strength from this kind of experience.

How much goes unsaid between men—the need to be mentored, nurtured, taught stories. The older men raise their heads a little higher as the younger men acknowledge them and ask them questions about their lives. The younger men see their lives spread out before them, and feel their love for their fathers, some for the first time since they were infants.

As the baby is passed around the circle, the unspoken promises of each member of this tribe are passed, from heart to hands: the promise to educate, to recognize, to share stories. The baby has been welcomed to the earth by a tribe.

The women stand in a circle around the men, weeping, moved to see the men express these ancient feelings. They strain to hear the words that are quietly spoken by their fathers, brothers, husbands, and male friends. The mother of this baby feels her body relax as she witnesses the multi-generational bonding of this sacred circle. This child's emotional and spiritual education will not rest upon her and her husband's shoulders alone. There is a tribe to help, to hold, support and nurture this new life.

You might think this gathering had taken place in the Serengeti Plains, or that it was part of the life of the native people of America. It might surprise you to learn that the grandfather and son in the circle are both attorneys in Boston. The rest of the circle was comprised of business professionals, doctors, CEO's, college students, retirees, artists, shop keepers, teachers, a carpentry contractor, and two entrepreneurs. It might also surprise you that most of these people live within twenty miles of their homes and businesses. This tribal circle took place in Newport, Rhode Island, but it could just as well have gathered anywhere there were people.

What would bring a group of people like this out of their busy, dedicated lives to stand and take part in this circle? It is the longing to participate in life in deeply meaningful ways, the inspiration and hope that the very living of our lives would lead us to our greatest potential, the sense of belonging to each other and to the mystery of life.

The Consequences Of Living Without Tribe

Everywhere we go, we meet people who feel they are running as fast as they can, yet they can't keep up, much less get ahead. They can't find the energy to be creative or to be inspired. Often they fall into bed at night with much of what they felt they needed to do left undone. We find the same frustrations, the same bewilderment and disappointment with life wherever we go.

It isn't that we have bitten off more than we can chew, or that our visions are greater than our capacity. Rather, our lives have become increasingly demanding because we are trying to do it all alone. We have forgotten that when we bring ourselves together to serve a common purpose, we each become capable of accomplishing more than we can as individuals. Instead of needing to be all things to all people and situations, we need to be committed to what is unique in us; when we bring our talents and capacities together with others, we can meet all the demands of living together, with time left for inspiration and play.

NAMING THE INTANGIBLE

When I (Jodi) first began to participate in tribal circles, I didn't even know to call them that. I knew only that I wanted my life, in some way, to be meaningful. I wanted to be part of a sharing and a way of life that mattered, a way to make sense of my life. I'd entertained fantasies about joining the Peace Corps. I'd dreamed of living in Bali, or going back to India, where I'd experienced a sense of belonging. But I am a Western woman. I live here and struggle with my loneliness here.

Now, as I stand in circles like the one described above, hearing people's life stories, reading their poetry, and witnessing their courage, my own walls fall away. Life begins making sense. My loneliness dissolves, and I remember that I do belong to something—I belong to life, to the human tribe.

Many of us feel tribe in the stirrings of our souls, connecting us with our ancient ancestors who lived in villages, and who depended on one another for growing and gathering food. They engaged in rituals to celebrate new life, to mourn the dead, to welcome the springtime, and to honor the spirits of life. Although we can never go back to that simpler way of life, we can once again embrace the values of the tribe, wherein we honor each other and the natural forces that support life.

The many stories and anecdotes presented here are of people who are no different than you and I. They live regular lives, have the same frustrations and joys, and are doing their best to meet the same kinds of challenges that confront us all. They are people who have discovered the power of practicing tribal values, who have stepped forward, honoring a thirst to educate themselves and each other in emotional, spiritual, and personal realms. They are people who are dissolving the painful illusions of separation that psychologists and spiritual teachers have identified as the tragedy of our times.

WHAT'S THIS BOOK ABOUT?

This book is about tribal revival. The longing to belong, and to have our lives make a difference. It's a map for a new way of living, bringing back the sacred into daily life.

This book is the collective voice of eleven years of tribe, with all the beauty of people's stories, quests, and risks. It is the collective heartbeat of many individuals who are living from a deep sense of purpose. It is the story of people who want their lives to be expressions of the sacred.

Over the past eleven years of our teaching and tribal gatherings, the term "sacred tribe" has emerged. For most, this term refers to the values and practices that create personal and spiritual connectedness. Year after year these values set the foundation for consciously alive tribal communities in every area of our lives: family, work, neighborhoods, intimate relationships, and personal development.

A CALL TO PARTICIPATE

We are two women who have longed for tribe. Out of our longing, we offer this book as one way of sharing the wisdom we have been so privileged to witness and be a part of. We offer these pages as a guide, as inspiration.

When you have finished reading this book you may find yourself moved to express your new tribal knowledge. You might, for example, find that you want to mentor someone at your workplace, to pass on your knowledge as a gift and invest yourself in someone else's development. Maybe you will find modest rituals in your daily life to bring honor and meaning to simple things. For instance, you might start each morning with a ritual of gratitude. Or perhaps within your family or larger communities you will gather to more fully recognize each other, and honor the human bonds you share in a tribal sense.

We hope you will feel the stirrings of your own longing and love of life, and through the reading of this book know and experience that your life is already valuable and full of meaning.

Our fondest hope would be that the stories you read will help you find your place within your existing tribes. You'll find in these pages countless examples of how others, from all walks of life, have successfully made this move in their lives. In the true tribal process that these stories represent, you will see ways that you are already expressing sacred tribal values, and you'll go on to expand these values into other areas of your life.

This book contains the collective wisdom of our very real and alive tribal community that has been learning and studying together for over eleven years. At the end of each chapter you will find their voices in the section called "Voices of The Tribe." The stories and anecdotes are real. Only some of the names have been changed.

If you were to ask any of the members what tribe they were from, they would undoubtedly answer, "the tribe of humanity, of life." In our communities, people come and go. What defines this broad and varied tribe is not that we live together—in fact, we are spread all over the world—but that each of us practices sacred tribal values in daily life. While any member of this tribe might or might not show up for an organized gathering or workshop, each of us practices these values in the context of our own lives, communities and work places, creating sacred tribe everywhere we go.

As you read this book, we hope you'll feel moved to practice the values we describe here.[1] And if you do, we hope that your life will be enriched, as ours has been through doing these practices. In traditional Hawaiian social structures it was understood that someone was part of the village "tied by ancestry, birth, and sentiment."[2] If you feel that sentiment with the voices that are woven together in this book . . . welcome to our village!

I

A CALL TO THE SACRED

When a man goes out into the night sky and looks up at the universe and does not feel a sense of awe at this unfolding mystery and a sense of intelligence greater than his own, he is already dead, but they have not buried him yet.
—*Albert Einstein*

Until we accept the fact that life itself is founded in the mystery, we shall learn nothing.
—*Henry Miller*

ONCE, WE (Carole and Jodi) spent a day in a Hmong village in Thailand, just sitting in one spot, watching. At daybreak the first women awoke, tended their fires, and began preparing food. A baby cried and a mother strapped him on her back. Another woman brought her baby to her breast. Women washed the youngest children, and older children helped. Men gathered their tools to work in the fields. As younger boys of the tribe stood at the village gate and looked on, the adolescents went with the men into the fields.

That afternoon, we sat with several young girls watching an older girl of about fourteen weaving magnificent strands of cotton—magenta, fuchsia, yellow, and turquoise—for the garment she would wear at her wedding.

In the course of the day stories were told, simple rituals were performed, children were disciplined, and occasionally tempers flared. We saw the young help and pay respect to the elders. Older children mentored and taught younger ones. We saw women in all stages of pregnancy and witnessed how the sick were cared for. A medicine man sacrificed two chickens and a bottle of whiskey for a person who was particularly ill. We listened to the laughter as families gathered at dusk to share the evening meal. And when the dinner was done, we joined with the entire village as they sat in a circle to tell stories, in a room lit with a single kerosene lamp. They listened intently as the chief spoke, and shared intimate exchanges. The adults gave the children time to frolic and be loved through the tribe's enjoyment of them. At the end of the evening, the women danced their ancestral dance, one that had been performed for hundreds of years, a dance telling the story of the tribe and its lineage.

This is tribe! But this kind of experience gets lost as we live further away from each other, sealed from our neighbors, hidden behind closed doors.

When asked that evening to share our ancestral dance, we realized we had none.

WHAT'S BEEN LOST?

Why does the word "tribe" move so many of us in these modern times when the word itself seems so archaic? Why does it stir a deep longing within us? Why does it move our souls, causing us to reach out to something that we can barely see rising out of the mist? In fleeting moments we experience a resonance with something very old and deep. We might describe it to ourselves as a feeling of peace, or of coming home, of being in harmony, or being complete and whole.

We may find such epiphanies at the top of a mountain in Thailand, but they are also available to us in Western life—in our families, corporations, in the privacy of our own struggles. Let's imagine for a moment that we could live much like the Hmong tribe we have described. What would we then have in the fabric of our existence that seems so rare and elusive to us today?

We would watch our elders grapple with things we hadn't yet grown into. We would have a deep appreciation for their wide and rich range of wisdom, from which we might one day draw. We would witness each and every stage of life, from birth, through adolescence, into adulthood. When the river of life brought us to that eddy, we would be prepared for that part of the journey. We would be educated through observing and participating in the tribe.

Tribe provides us with a community that can love and make room for every member to be who he or she actually is. It is a place where we are celebrated for who we are, for our innate gifts and wisdom.

The wisdom that comes with simply witnessing others is profound. I (Jodi) remember being in a hot tub with Carole when she was seven months pregnant. As an adult woman, I had never seen a pregnant woman's body. I was amazed to see what a woman's body can actually do! I immediately thought of my mother—she must have looked like that too! Of course I already knew this somewhere in my mind, but my sense of my self as a woman, my body, my mother, all women, was changed in the presence of The Great Mother that day.

Such moments would be no less magical in the tribe except that the experience of a woman's body and the feminine archetypes would be a part of one's everyday life, from an early age.

PART OF A LARGER WHOLE

We like to imagine a member of the Hmong tribe whispering in our ears at times when we are struggling to make sense of life. This tribesman might tell stories or recount what he had seen his brother or grandfather do during similar times of challenge or crisis. We imagine his coaching would provide us with insight and a new way of seeing the situation.

Watching. That's such an important concept in tribe. Through watching we learn that each stage of life is whole and gives way to the next. The village life gives us a mandala, a big-picture perspective, each tribe member playing an important role. The truth is that we already take part in a continuum that extends beyond our own life spans. We are all part of an evolving process, one that is never finished. Tribe allows us to see our part in the eternal flow more clearly, to be inspired by it, to be shown how our lives have meaning far beyond the reach of our own years. In the context of tribal learning, we find ourselves part of something larger than ourselves. Not just a part of God, which can be difficult for us to imagine, but part of a work in progress which mirrors back the evolution of human consciousness.

In modern life, the absence of tribe causes a hunger that can't be fulfilled by modern palliatives: more activity, more relationships, more gadgets to entertain us, more goals to achieve. Along with losing our tribal vocabulary—us, we, our, offer, share, open, receiving, giving—we have lost our connection to each other, to humanity, and to the planet. We cling to the vision that life is about me and mine, about here and now. We begin to feel that we are alone, isolated from the eternal flow of life.

When we can see ourselves as part of a larger whole, one that extends beyond our own life spans into the infinity of the cosmos, our singular lives take on meaning. This connects us to the continuum that many spiritual teachers urge us to seek—our relationship to the force of life itself.

TECHNOLOGY AND SEPARATION

Through technology we have dissolved geographic boundaries that once divided us, and our world gets smaller every day. Through airplanes, radio, television, satellites, telephones, and new computer technologies, there is hardly a place on our planet that is isolated from the rest. News travels at the speed of light. The grandsons and granddaughters of Q'ero elders, living at 20,000 feet up in the Andes, listen to rock 'n roll music broadcast to their Walkman radios via satellite. Tibetan monks in the Himalayas press cell phones to their ears to confer with supporters in Europe and the United States. A tribesman in the Amazon hovers over a short wave radio, talking to a trader in Mexico City.

With this kind of access to the whole world, it would seem that we were becoming one big tribe. Yet this is not the case. We are more partitioned, more isolated than ever before. The breakdown of our tribal connections is not found in geographic distances, but in our consciousness. While it is true that we have physical access to one another, we have abandoned the outer rituals and teachings that demonstrate how to be with one another.

I (Carole) lived on a hilltop before my son was born. I loved the view and the trees, the privacy and the quiet. Once my son was born I wanted to move to a neighborhood with lawns and kids. It took a while to adjust, but now I enjoy it when the neighbor boys hop the fence. I come home to find them in my yard playing, in my kitchen getting a bowl of cereal. Yet still, I don't feel that I truly *know* my neighbors. Something keeps us separate.

In modern life, *knowing* our neighbors usually means little more than that we know their names. And if our kids go to the same school, maybe we've discussed our children over a cup of coffee at a school function. But tribal experiences teach us that there's much more to knowing each other.

There is a wonderful story about a writer who went to visit a tribe living in the Kalahari Desert. This journalist intended to live among them and study their customs. One day he asked one of the tribe members, "Do you like your neighbor?" The village man replied, "Do I like my neighbor?" And left it at that. Many days went by, until at last the tribesman gestured to the reporter, "Come with me." And he took the reporter across the dirt path to his neighbor's hut. There the journalist and two tribesmen sat for the better part of the day, talking and laughing. Day after day, the tribesman would take the reporter and they'd visit the neighbor. Some days they would hunt, some days they'd stay in the village. This went on for several weeks, until finally, the tribesman sat down with the reporter and said, "You asked me if I liked my neighbor. There, that is how I feel about my neighbor." Where we might have expected a short answer from this tribesman, "yes, I do," or "no, I don't," we were instead invited in to experience the actual beauty and substance of that friendship.

So, I don't know my neighbors. We are friendly. I like them. But I do not know them. The boundaries of our homes are clearly delineated by our walls and shrubs and property lines. I have never cooked with the woman next door. I have never watched her discipline her children or comfort them when they cry. I don't know what the husband felt during the breakup of his first marriage, what he looks like when he is struggling to solve a problem, grappling with defeat, or how he expresses his love. And since I do not know my neighbors, I have no access to who and what they truly are. We can't learn from one another, pool our resources or our wisdom, or enact the rites and rituals that bring deeper meaning into daily life. Living so closely, one might expect more, but members of the same tribe we are not.

It's not only property lines and walls that prevent us from more deeply connecting with one another. The distance we're concerned with in this book is one that we've created by putting greater and greater physical and psychological distances between ourselves and the sources of our basic needs. For example, millions of children growing up in the cities and suburbs have no concept of how the food they eat is grown, or how it gets to the market. Younger couples eat at least half their meals in restaurants. This separation from the sources of our food supports an illusion that we have much more control of our destiny, and therefore much less need for tribe, than is truly the case.

Ask a Kalahari tribesman where his food comes from and he'll probably take you out on a hunt, or suggest that you spend the next few days gathering wild melons, herbs, and native root crops with the women. In the process, you'd learn about the terrain, when things were ready to pick, how to harvest what you needed without damaging the plant or surrounding environs. If hunting, you'd learn to track, to recognize small signs that tell you an animal is near, the names and legends of certain creatures encountered along the way. Mostly, you'd learn about the close relationship between yourself, other tribe members, and the Earth. You'd touch the sacred each time you harvested a vegetable or fruit, or tracked, killed, and dressed a game animal.

What a contrast this is to the modern world of supermarkets and malls, of electronic shopping, of transacting business from computer and modem, and of even having sexual experiences in cyberspace.

SURVIVAL OF THE TRIBAL SPIRIT

Can our tribal yearnings survive when we are surrounded by the daily pressures and temptations of modern life? There is evidence that tribal consciousness is universal, that it endures in the human soul regardless of its diminished expressions. We see it manifest in the Million Man and Million Woman Marches, in the Christian Men's Movement, and in new trends of urban housing, such as co-housing. We find it in mothers' groups, in support groups that address issues as far-ranging as addiction and conscious dying. We find tribal consciousness in the formation of corporate team management groups that emphasize spiritual values in the work place. It's even expressed in the youth gangs of the inner city. It's often these "fringe groups" of society that tip us off to the needs of the larger society.

Clearly, there is an undeniable need to feel that we are part of a larger reality, something that extends beyond building our families, our careers, our bank accounts, and our real estate holdings. Many people feel this instinctual yearning for tribe, yet can't identify what it is. They may not be drawn to one of these groups, perhaps because they have no overt need, no addiction, aren't a minority, aren't a parent in need of support, or aren't in group therapy.

From our experiences working with thousands of people in our workshops, one need stands out—it is the need for closer connections with each other, for a feeling that our own lives matter to other people, and that others lives matter to us.

As a society we are desperate for something we may have not yet identified. But we must name it—our survival depends on it. Western culture has come to a turning point. Up until now we have been motivated by the quest for power and accomplishments in the material world. But we have reached the apex of that developmental cycle in human evolution, and those outer props are no longer enough to shore up the vessel of human consciousness. Like a human being at mid-life, we are a society at mid-passage, seeking rites and rituals. We know this both as individuals and as a society. We know that our values are changing. We are entering a new phase. Like all creatures in transition, we must release ourselves from old values that no longer work for us, and be available to new ones that serve.

DO WE HAVE TO LIVE TOGETHER?

Who among us would give up our freedom in order to return to a collective lifestyle such as that of the Hmong people? Probably not many of us. But there is a different direction we can take to reclaim our tribal bonds. This one requires not so much a change of place or lifestyle as a change in our consciousness. And this change leads us to incorporate new behaviors and practices into our lives, initiating a way of relating to and being in the world that opens our minds to our tribal links, and giving us ways to rebuild them.

This tribal consciousness is no doubt connected with those inner impulses for survival that have been with us since the dawn of time. Long ago that instinctual urge was woven into the fabric of daily existence, and people could clearly see and feel the patterns. Together they built barriers against marauding neighbors. They cultivated crops and domesticated animals so that their basic needs would be met. They divided up the labor within their gates and kept the roles clearly defined, knowing that if they were to maintain their united strength each person had to do their individual part.

There was a price that the people paid for that interweaving process. They didn't have the freedom to travel, the freedom to change their roles in society at midstream, the freedom to leave the village and go out on their own. Today, we're all aware of the fact that we have gained many riches from our ability to move away from the tribe. But we're reaching the limits of our exploration of individualization, and life's pendulum is swinging back to center.

The sacred retribalization we explore in this book does not require us to go back in time to simpler, more elemental ways. It does demand a willingness to take our places in society as contributing members, to be responsible for the impact of our choices on those around us, and on our planet. It requires learning about the sacred values that are at the heart of human existence. Above all, this new tribal consciousness evolving out of the mist asks us to open ourselves to our sacred nature and the mysteries of life.

There's a story about a man named Manny who every morning and every evening dropped to his knees, prostrated himself, and pleaded, "God, I am so poor, please let me win the lottery. It doesn't even have to be a big one. Anything will help."

Many years pass. Each day is the same. Manny drops to his knees to pray. But never hearing his name announced at the lottery, he grows frustrated and exasperated.

At last, dejected, broken, and feeling betrayed, he drops to his knees and cries, "Really God, I have believed in you and served you all my life. Can't you give me just this one little proof that you exist? Is it such a big thing?" There is a long moment of silence, and the poor man falls to the ground in a heap, defeated and forlorn. But suddenly, he hears a booming voice echoing over the land. It is God, no doubt about it!

"Manny," God says, "you've got to help me out a little, here."

"Anything!" Manny replies.

"Just this," God says. "Buy a ticket!"

This lesson seems laughably obvious. Many of us want the benefits of community, but we somehow can't connect this desire with actions that make it happen. So how do we buy a ticket, and what might it cost?

THE PRICE OF A TICKET

A friend described a new approach to juvenile crime in a small, northern California town. We know that juvenile crime affects the whole community. It is costly to rehabilitate young offenders, and the rehabilitation rarely works; when it doesn't, we end up with the child's behavior becoming increasingly antisocial, costing us all money and grief. While many juveniles turn to criminal behavior because they lack a feeling of connection with a "tribe," our traditional way of treating them is to cast them even further out, rather than taking them into the fold.

Instead of immersing the offender in the criminal justice system, the counselors of this small town bring the offender together with his victims. Through sometimes arduous counseling on both sides, an agreement is worked out for the perpetrator to make retribution to his victims. Where money or material damages are involved, a perpetrator might help the injured party paint their house or build a fence. Where bodily injury is involved, the offender might be required to hear about the emotional and physical pain they inflicted, and combine this counseling with volunteer work at a trauma center where he could witness first hand the suffering of people who are hurt, and even dying.

Instead of being jailed, where the offender joins hands with a "criminal tribe," the perpetrator learns about the human impact of his own deeds—good and bad. In the process of making retribution he has an opportunity to reclaim his own pride and dignity, to be included in a healthy tribe, valued and nurtured. He may even have an opportunity to heal some of his own wounds, wounds that may have contributed to his misbehavior. He begins to experience himself as a contributor rather than a thief, a renegade, or a tough guy standing alone. Many victims and perpetrators in this program have become friends, with bitterness and grief giving way to forgiveness, love and a new sense of belonging to community, of taking an important part in the tribe.

What we describe here is a radical example of the sacred tribal way brought from the past into modern life. It is an ancient way of reclaiming members who have been disconnected from the tribe, a practice that has existed for thousands of years in tribal societies where imprisoning or executing offenders was unheard of because it was recognized how acts of punishment could divide and weaken a tribe.

We know that tribal consciousness can be created in every aspect of our lives—in our marriages, in the work place, in our families, in the larger communities to which we belong, and even in special groups that we establish to explore these values and practices. What we create in our individual lives can extend out into tribal connections that embrace our entire planet and, in turn, embrace us individually.

We know that as we learn to hold tribal consciousness within our own hearts, we automatically develop a sense of purpose, compassion, self-love and self-respect, and joyfully offer it to the world. Tribal consciousness starts first within our own hearts. It is a shift in perception, with a focus on the sacred.

THE SACRED IN EVERYDAY LIFE

For some people, the word "sacred" brings up religious impressions that may or may not be inviting. For others, there may be a sense of the holy or arcane that seems inaccessible. As we use the word here, sacred involves the values that connect us to the deeper meaning of life.

I (Jodi) remember wandering around Bangkok during my first trip to Asia, and watching people buying food to bring home for dinner, or seeing adolescent boys eating together at a food stand. All this was taking place at the base of the steps to the temple, the temple in full view, rising towards the sky. I often think of this image to remind myself that the sacred is everywhere; all of life is sacred. The sacred is the call to enter life fully and authentically. We can find that invitation everywhere in daily life. We simply have to recognize it. Everyday life events and situations take on vivid definition, color, and meaning when viewed from the perspective of the sacred.

Until recent history, we were reminded of the sacred through myths, folk stories, spiritual teachings, and through tribal rituals. We depended on these to keep alive our awareness of the mystery and our consciousness of a power greater than ourselves. Tribal life, and the link it offers us with the continuum that stretches way beyond our life span, teaches us that we are the expression of the sacred mysteries, and that our sacred practices are the threads that lead us back home to God. The sacred provides us with a map to the universe, to God, one that existed long before we came into this life, and will exist long after we are gone. It is through the sacred that our lives become connected to something deeper, richer and more fulfilling.

We can explore ways to renew this sense of awe, this reverence for the mystery, not by returning to a more primitive lifestyle, or necessarily by living communally, but through finding in ourselves the spirit of communion with life, remembering that living is not a problem to be solved but an unfolding mystery to be experienced.

GOALS VERSUS MEANING

If we're to understand the sacred and its role in our search for a new tribal order, we need to be clear about the difference between "goal" and "meaning." In contemporary life, we've blurred the distinctions between these two. For instance, what gives our lives a sense of meaning in early adulthood includes things like owning a new car, having a good job, and getting married. But while these may contain meaning for us, they are actually goals.

If we at last achieve our goals, there's usually a period when we feel relatively satisfied. If we don't achieve our goals, or only partially achieve them, then we either quit or intensify our efforts to fulfill them. Regardless of what happens, however, there comes a time when we feel that our lives lack meaning—a deeper, more intimate connection to life. Because we have not learned to distinguish between goals and meaning, we can seek to satisfy our need by establishing new goals or trying harder to achieve old ones. This leads to a sense of impotence and despair, since we can never find meaning if we are only seeking the fulfillment of goals. We end up being like the proverbial drunk who seeks his lost keys under the lamp post, not because that is where he dropped them, but because the light is better there.

To clarify the difference between goals and meaning, we share the following anecdote:

Let's suppose you have never played golf and have decided you want to start. You go to a golf course, find a pro and you ask, "Okay, what's the goal?"

The pro's reply is simple enough. "The goal is to get the ball in the hole."

So far, so good. You pick up a ball, walk over to the hole and drop it in.

"There, mission accomplished. I got the ball in the hole," you exclaim.

"Well," the pro says, "that's not exactly it. You have to get the ball in the hole, but to get it there you must beat it with a stick. Not only that, the person who beats the ball the most loses."

"Ah," you think, "there seems to be more to this than just getting the ball in the hole."

And there is much more. The game itself is about your body, the instruments you are using, the configuration of the land, the wind, the weather, your general state of mind when you play, who you're playing with, and the fates. It is about all the relationships that transpire along the way, to the stroke that sinks the ball in the final hole.

Living in a state separated from tribe, we too easily slip into a goal-oriented way of life. We start thinking that there is an inevitable end, an absolute apex, an ultimate goal. Modern society offers an endless array of goals—the house in the suburbs, the happy marriage, the perfect job or profession, the dream of living without experiencing the discomforts of anxiety, grief, conflict, or doubt. If we just stay on track and do it right, or do it enough, we will be rewarded with the golden trophy at the end of the game.

We imagine there is a payoff that will make all our sacrifices, all the miseries we've endured up to that point, worth all the effort. We beat the daylights out of the little white ball, driving it to the last hole, bruising our hands, enduring fits of frustration with the hope that in the end, when we finally sink the last ball in the last hole, our lives will be complete and joyful. At last we'll have enough love, enough money, enough self-esteem and enough achievements. Will we, though?

When the values of the tribe are missing, and the sacred values are either neglected or unknown to us, our lives easily become meaningless, a string of individual goals and acts with no link to a deeper guiding force. A wonderful question to ask yourself is, "At the end of my life, looking back at all that I've experienced, what is it that I will have valued the most?" The very question itself brings us into the realm of the sacred. What is the unseen force that connects and gives meaning to all of life's actions? The sacred is the magic, the alchemical ingredient that lifts and heightens us, inspires us to move beyond the limitations of our ordinary lives. Sacred values are the values that link us to deeper meaning, beyond the temporal boundaries of our physical existence, connecting us with the great mysteries.

We all want to belong, to have meaning, to be connected to life in deep ways. We long to have our lives count, to feel that we matter. While we have never met a person who hasn't experienced this yearning at some time in their life, we have met people who long ago stopped believing it was possible. We have met people who forgot this feeling or shoved it into the background, denying it to themselves, thinking that perhaps it was arrogant of them to even entertain such a possibility, believing it was something that only "special" people enjoyed. But inevitably, with a little nudge, even those who are loudest in their denial reconnect with their desire for this sacred intent. Eventually, we all discover that this connection is the underpinning of our lives.

We may get distracted for a while. But once we can voice that longing, we begin to realize we can do something about it. Connection doesn't just happen one day, though. We need to *buy the ticket,* as the story about our friend Manny instructs. We need to ask ourselves, "How am I participating in my life? What am I contributing?" Asking these questions will lead us to the actions that buy the ticket, the ticket to the lottery that is our own lives, where the prize is our own souls.

RECLAIMING OUR SACRED IDENTITY

I (Carole) remember going to camp one summer of my adolescence. It was a summer of shame—about myself, my body, my youthful awkwardness. I had no place to fit in. I knew I couldn't turn to my home for support. The pain and isolation I felt there was overwhelming. I longed for something I did not have, arms to hold myself in love.

One day I went for a walk. It was a day when my despair was greatest and my anguish fullest. At the end of the walk I lay down on the grass. Even to this day I remember the first sensations of my whole being beginning to dissolve. For a moment I panicked. I was literally dissolving into the earth, the sky, into tiny molecules and atoms, losing the boundaries I'd come to recognize as myself. I was becoming a part of everything. As this happened, I began to feel a deep experience of love. I instantly recognized all of life in a new way. I knew every blade of grass, the sky, the trees, each person who passed through my awareness. I knew without words that everything was a part of this immense unconditional love, and that this love took many forms, many shapes, but everything was essentially the same. I knew, without the confirmation of conceptual thought, that my existence was purposeful. And I knew I was somehow an important part of this love, in all its forms of human struggle and emotion, and that to finally dissolve one day back into this love was good.

When I began coming out of this state, I knew I would dedicate my life to bringing this vision, this state of being, more fully into my consciousness. I knew my purpose was to make it accessible to myself and others. I was left that summer with a deep feeling of love and union, with everyone and everything around me. I imagined that everyone older than me also had such experiences, and that I would meet those who could name this path and help me more fully connect with it. I was fourteen years old that summer. I waited many years to find others with whom I could discuss what I had experienced.

At fourteen, I imagined that I would begin meeting people who would sit with me, who would support me in my education, who would help me to understand more about what I had envisioned at camp that summer. I imagined an education of my soul and my spiritual growth, an education of myself as a woman and a human being living with the earth. I imagined an education in which my personality would be molded to walk in alignment with my greater purpose in love, as a being capable of expressing, enacting, and living the deeper mystery into which I had stumbled. I imagined there would be rites and rituals to be learned. I would be taught to be a productive, contributing member of society, of clan, of family.

Instead, life went on as usual. At camp there was swimming and archery, squabbles in the dorms, and finally the journey back home to an even more meaningless existence. As time passed, I discovered I could stay in touch with the deep feelings of love, and the unshakable knowledge that nothing exists outside God. But I couldn't believe that nobody around me talked about these things. I couldn't understand why the outer goals of my life were the only things that were valued.

In our undefined hunger for the tribal connection we instinctively know that there is more to life than we can see and measure in external events, goals, and accomplishments. We recognize that there is a spiritual emptiness in our lives, within our souls, that we do not know how to fill. If we're willing, we open our minds to the possibility that the pain and longing of this emptiness is the compass for charting our way out of the dark wilderness in which we've become lost. It can show us the way back to our tribal dwelling.

There is something in the word tribe that suggests a reason, a purpose for our existence. From the feelings that are raised as we think about tribe comes a very essential question: "Why bother to do my life at all if it doesn't serve a larger cause, if it doesn't make a contribution, if it doesn't add something that can make our existence a little better? Why bother if in my life I feel increasingly separate from my soul, my family, my community, and from the earth itself?"

What is tribe if not that wondrous, clear container, like a magnificent mountain pool, that mirrors back to us all the sacred parts of ourselves? Tribe helps us to remember our love and our important place in life. It helps us know and understand and live in harmony with life, with what life calls us to do. It links us with the fact that there is a greater purpose than ourselves. Imagine a gathering, a tribe, where the events of daily life, birth and death, the movement from infancy to childhood, from childhood to adolescence, and so on up through our deaths, are honored and respected. We can each begin to take steps to humanize our lives through the restoration of tribal consciousness. This is our rich inheritance of being.

Voices Of The Tribe

At night there are millions of galaxies; the sky shimmering alight with fire. I lie on my back gazing into the infinity, questioning my place in this vastness. There is something that I know when I look at the night sky. I know why I love, why I feel connected to life in all its forms. I feel blessed and whole, part of all people, plants, animals, and the earth. When I gaze at the night sky I feel in awe of the hugeness of life. When I gaze at the night sky I feel love, loving through me. I feel both meaningful and insignificant. I feel the smallness and largeness of life all in one millisecond. I long to stay connected to my passion for living that comes with these awakenings. I love moments like this, when I can contain the opposites, when I feel invincible because the force of life holds me in its palms.

—Lily Myers

From a man who is HIV positive:

In my life I choose to partake fully of every experience offered me and those created by my own volition. I intend to not let fear ever stop me, kill me, beat me. I will walk into every day with an awesome understanding of the power of the magnificence I am; the empowerment of the soul life force; the greatness of my being created and loved by God. Re-created and loved by my family, my friends, the earth, the animals, the heavens...and myself. The absolute totality of joy and the bittersweet understanding of pain

*will meld solidly within my heart to give me the strength to believe and
comprehend that life is a balance of all that was, is, and will be. To cherish
each day by embracing the gift of unconditional love for myself and others.*

—Rick Garza

*Welcome to my world
Where boundaries vanish into the heavens
Where a lifetime happens in a single minute
And a minute lasts forever.*

*Come join me in my world
Where every inhale says I love you
Where every glance and parting of the lips
Speak of all there is to say.*

*I love living in this world
Where truth has a podium to speak from
Desire has a stage to dance on
And I have room to grow.*

*Will you meet me in this world
Where the silence brings intimacy
Our unspoken words ring out their laughter
And the ear of our bodies hears music that has always played.*

—Deborah Heller

2

A Call For Living Tribe

There is a way in which the collective knowledge of
mankind expresses itself... through mere daily living: a way
in which life itself is sheer knowing.
            —*Laurens Van der Post*

There are seasons in human affairs, of inward and outward
revolution, when new depths seem to be broken up in the
soul, when new wants are unfolded in multitudes, and a
new and undefined good is thirsted for....
            —*William Ellery Channing*

HOW DO WE begin to renew our tribal links? We start with
an understanding that the wisdom inherent in areas such as
the Hmong village is not an invented wisdom. Rather, it is
a body of knowledge drawn from living life, made up of universal
truths, truths that are constant for all times and all peoples. They are
true whether you are living in a bustling city or in a remote village
cut off from the modern world. They are true whether you are a
pauper or the richest person on earth. And they are as true today as
they were 500 years ago.

We can each begin learning these truths for ourselves—the
tools are far more accessible than you might think. We get in touch
with this wisdom through stories such as the ones contained in this
book, and through the kinds of exercises you'll find in Part Three.

In Hmong village life, every passage of human existence is
taking place out from behind closed doors. A wisdom evolves from

these experiences that offers a focused, concentrated, and complete picture of life. For members of the Hmong tribe, daily living demands an awareness of one another at all times. Each individual knows the strength he draws from the tribe, his dependence on the tribe, and is keenly aware of the importance of supporting and nurturing the tribe. From this awareness comes a natural instinct and desire to serve. Through the everyday rituals of life, members are connected with forces unseen. The sacredness of life is avowed with each breath, even the simplest actions declaring our human ties with the mystery, with that invisible spirit from which we all come.

When confronted with conflict, illness, the beginning of a new passage or the end of an old one, nothing seems askew or even unfamiliar to the Hmong people. Because they live openly, as a tribe, they have exactly what they need to take on life's challenges and changes. All living is the source of their wisdom. The Hmong know what to expect in so many of life's situations. When they have a baby, get married, or suffer the loss of a loved one, they are automatically offered the support and wisdom of the tribe. There is always someone nearby who has been through it themselves, so that as the next person goes through the same thing, they have already seen the map. The wisdom and experience of the collective body of the tribe nurtures and strengthens the spirit of every individual member. And from the strength of each individual the tribe itself is nourished, and nourishes others in return.

In tribal life, having our hearts and minds—indeed, our very souls!—open to the tribe's vast pool of experience and wisdom provides all we need. Out of tribal living there evolves an inherent understanding that we are one. Our strength and happiness come from service and our contribution to the larger whole. Through this offering, we feel the tribal impulse that each of us inherits at birth. Little by little, we begin to see the path to tribal consciousness that has been there all along.

There is a wonderful passage from Caryn Lea Summers' book, *Circle of Health,* that reminds us of these invisible connections that we learn to see as we recover our tribal selves. Summers says: "I envision the universe as a vast wheel, which represents shared consciousness. Each of us is at a different point on the wheel, but we are all moving in the same direction. Although we are all on separate paths, our destination is the same."[1]

Surely our longing for tribal connection comes from a part of us that recognizes this shared consciousness, an awareness that is timeless, a cellular memory, if you will, that by now must be as if carried by a special gene or perhaps in the blood. When we are guided by our elders and our spiritual teachers, feelings that are deep and primordial remind us that we, too, are members of the tribe of humanity. Though we may have temporarily forgotten the skills that connect us, we know how important they are and how immutable is our need for a sense of belonging.

Tribal living tells us to throw open the doors which we have shut in response to contemporary life. By observing life's vast panorama close up, and fully participating in it, our experiences of life become rich and fertile, instructive and uplifting, far more fulfilling than any life we might have created in isolation. Even when confronted with conflicts, complications, and grief, there is a sense of engagement and exhilaration. When things go wrong or get difficult, we don't take it as a personal failing. Rather, we know from our own experience that life is rich, varied and constantly going through cycles. As life in tribe moves through all its natural cycles, we respond openly, flowing with the changes. We discover, as Joseph Campbell once said, that "we are a match for the world and the world is a match for us."

The good news is that we do not have to abandon modern life and go to live with a tribe like the Hmong to reclaim our connection with the sacredness of life. This is the main message of our book. Instead, we can consciously create new ways of looking at our daily lives as they are. Where do we begin with such a venture? Well, the truth is that we are already doing this in our lives—we just haven't recognized it as such. And recognition is critical! As author Wayne Dyer said, "You'll see it when you believe it."

SEEING AND RECOGNITION

A man in one of our workshops told how he was teaching his young son about the celestial constellations. The father did everything he could think of in the hope that his son could look up into the heavens and see the Big Dipper, or Orion. He spent countless hours with him, lying on the ground at night looking up, but to no avail. The father even took black pieces of paper and punched holes in them in the patterns of the constellations. Shining a flashlight through the paper in a dark room, he would approximate for his son how the constellations would be seen in the night sky.

Then one evening, as he and his son were star-gazing, the boy leapt to his feet and pointed excitedly toward the sky. "There it is, that's the Big Dipper!" he cried.

The father turned to his son and said, "You finally see it!"

And the son replied, "No, Dad. I always saw it. But now I *recognize* it!"

The lesson for us here is that we are already immersed in the sacredness of life. In fact, it's impossible to escape it. Even so, we may not always be able to recognize it. Special rituals and celebrations can help us to recognize significant events in our lives and the life of our tribe. There are times when we need to stop our daily routines and say, "I feel this moment is important." And what are the significant events? Some obvious ones are birth celebrations, graduations from high school or college, engagements for marriage, and funerals, events that have an impact on the tribe.

I (Carole) remember the excitement of going to my friend's college graduation. At the age of forty-five she had decided to change the course of her life and become a psychotherapist. She had to keep working at her clerical job, so her course work took many years, but finally the day of her graduation arrived. She walked down the aisle in cap and gown, alongside other graduates in their twenties, a proud woman who would turn fifty that same month. For those who were her friends, it was a deeply moving moment of recognition, of honoring that sacred spirit of renewal which had carried my friend to a new way of life, and during a time when others her age were counting their years to retirement.

Every time we gather to honor and recognize our life passages, we bring a rich meaning to our lives. Tribe holds and gives form to this meaning and connection; it is the bridge to our awareness, to our full recognition that every moment of life is the expression of a larger whole, the invisible spirit that breathes life into every living being.

As a tribal participant, our regular involvement with life's flow can link us with truths that are far greater than the everyday goals and purposes we create for ourselves. We are linked with the sacred. Once we have recognized the sacred moments of tribal consciousness that occur in our lives, meaning, belonging, and connection naturally flow forth.

Like the boy who one day recognizes the Big Dipper that he had been seeing all along, we hope the insights and exercises in this book will enable you to recognize the sacred in your own lives. By looking at such moments in these new ways, each of us creates little templates, like the father did when he punched holes in black paper, that will allow us not just to see but to recognize the hidden constellations that are the sacred experiences of everyday life.

STRANGERS SHARE A LARGER TRUTH

Tribal consciousness is not limited to people who agree with our way of thinking. In fact, it is an awareness that we can experience with virtually everyone, even with people we barely know. A friend of ours, Mike, related to us a rather dramatic example of a moment when life unexpectedly allowed two people to recognize their sacred connection.

MIKE WAS DRIVING on a narrow mountain road in northern California one fall, hurrying home after a weekend of camping on the coast. The road he traveled was cut into the side of sharp cliffs, and on the west side of the road there were only flimsy metal wands separating traffic from a 200 foot drop into the Pacific surf.

Mike was driving fast. He came around a sharp turn to find a long line of oncoming traffic. Without warning, a red car pulled out of the line to pass, less than fifty yards ahead of Mike. Mike slammed on his brakes but saw that it was going to be impossible to stop in time. At the same moment, he spotted a narrow vista point between himself and the red car. Mike swerved out onto the gravel shoulder, but his front wheels hit loose dirt and his car spun out of control. His car hurtled sideways now, toward the edge of the cliff, then shuddered to a stop.

He opened his eyes. In front of him he saw the horizon high above the ocean. But his car was miraculously on solid ground, though only a few feet from the edge of the cliff! Taking a deep breath, he turned his head. The red car was alongside his own. It, too, had gone into a skid and the two vehicles had slid sideways into one another, actually touching but without causing damage to the metal. Mike saw the face of the other driver, his eyes wide with terror. For a long time the two men just stared at one another, speechless, emptied of all thoughts, acutely aware of having just escaped disaster.

The cars were so close together that the two men had to slide across and exit from the passenger sides of their cars. For a long time Mike and the stranger just stared at one another. The driver of the red car spoke first.

"That was so bloody stupid of me," he said, with a thick British accent. "You saved my damn life, man!"

"And you almost took mine," Mike said.

The two men stood facing one another for a long time, then suddenly they embraced, sobbing on each others' shoulders. Then, without another word, they got into their cars and drove off.

Over the next few days, Mike gave a great deal of thought to what had occurred that day. He was furious with the other driver for putting him at risk. Who could argue that this stranger had done something very stupid and dangerous! But all judgments aside, the bottom line was that they had both come very close to dying, and that event had reminded them of the preciousness of life. Regardless of the cause that put them in that position, something had allowed them to look into each other's faces and see their essential humanity. What they both touched that day was the sacred tribal bond that transcends even the most negligent or brutal act.

Sometimes the tribal connection is recognized with the exchange of just a few words, words that can nevertheless make a real difference in our lives. I (Carole) was reminded of this in the first months following my separation from my husband. I was on a business call and for some reason I mentioned to my caller that my husband had just moved out. There was a moment's pause, and then my business associate said, "Oh, I've been divorced twice. It's always painful. You're just in the beginning phases now, and it will take about two years for you to feel that your life is becoming normal again."

Those words rang a bell for me. At that moment, I recognized that grieving the end of what had been a primary relationship in my life would take time. Since then, I have thought about these words many times, particularly when I am feeling lost, wondering, "Why me? Why am I not over this yet? Why am I failing to move on as quickly as I'd like?" I remind myself that it has only been a year, and this important transition of my life has a predictable cycle and season. How do I know? Because others have come before me. They have traveled through this territory. Instead of hiding their pain and confusion, they have shared their stories with me, using their experiences to teach.

They didn't have to go to school to learn how to do this. Rather, they found their capacity for tribal connection in their willingness to be truthful and open, showing us how we can all be in tribe.

CHARTING SACRED GROUND

One day, for a women's workshop, I (Carole) asked Alice, who had been my nanny and my family's maid when I was a child, if she would come and just sit with the women. Alice had been very important to me. She lived graciously and beautifully, and her life was always an inspiration to me, though our lifestyles were very different. She would clean the house, cook, and iron, and she would just be with me. The days Alice came to our house, I followed her around like a puppy. And as I grew into womanhood and became a teacher, I began to realize that much of the wisdom I had came from her.

The day she came to sit with the women's group, she sat on a chair, white-haired, seventy-six years old. She couldn't fathom why I asked her to come. I told her that I just wanted the other women to meet her, to be able to ask questions and have her talk to them. I invited her not because she knew something special but because she was so beautifully open to life. I knew she would tell them of her life and of her feelings. And I knew that most, if not all, of the women had never just sat with an elder to simply *ask*.

They asked Alice how it felt to be a maid. They inquired about how it felt to be poor. They asked what it was like to have loved me while not actually being my mother. They asked how it felt to try and have a baby for years with no success, to enter menopause, to have her beloved husband, Otis, die. They wanted to know what it was like to grow old, to sit here with them and recognize that what she knew about living was important to others. They wanted to know what it had been like for Alice to grow up black in the South when life was segregated, how it felt to sit in the back of the bus. There was so much they wanted to know, and she answered. She simply answered from her heart with all the passion of what she had lived and felt. She did not tell them how to live, or what to do. More importantly, she related to them what she had lived. They listened, the whole group listened.

At dinner that night, I listened to the group as they talked about the events of that day. The conversations that evening had a new tone, one of permission; the women were now asking questions of each other and answering with their hearts. Alice changed us with her straight-forward honesty, and her generosity in sharing her life. We learned how to bring ourselves to each other, reclaiming the practices that create sacred tribe.

With the supportive experience of tribe, we are encouraged to step into life and live more fully. We are encouraged to be open and present with each moment of our lives. What happens, in part, is that instead of trying to control life, walling ourselves off from the parts we find unpleasant or fearful, we do just the opposite. We accept it all.

Modern life teaches us to insulate ourselves from much of life, making it possible for us to be highly productive. However, when illness strikes, or we lose a job, or we get into financial difficulty, or a child gets into trouble, life appears to be going crazy. Life seems to be out of control. We feel alone in our greatest moments of need because we have been shielded from the truth—that lots of other people go through the same things we're experiencing now. This invisibility can be devastating, because we never see other people face these problems. We don't know what's coming next, and as a result we're like children wandering in the wilderness. We ask questions such as, "Why is this happening to me? Where did I go wrong? How do I control this?"

Tribal living, by contrast, means fully opening ourselves to life. What we soon discover is that the more we can see, the more our anxieties about living fade away. We find solutions, alternatives. Our ideas about "quality of life" shift. As the walls come down, we open up not only to life's challenges but to life's wonders and joys.

A friend of ours, Dean, told us how he went through several years of hating to see people begging in the streets where he worked. He made harsh judgments about them, seeing them all as drug addicts, lazy and dysfunctional, a breed of animals that had nothing to do with him. One November, his fiancée, Trish, volunteered to help out at a soup kitchen that her church was sponsoring for the homeless. Dean was appalled. He could not imagine why Trish would want to do such a thing, and he told her he thought she was nuts. A big argument ensued, which ended with Trish saying, "I'll tell you why I'm going to do it. Because they are human beings just like you and me."

Dean looked at Trish in amazement. How could she possibly compare her own life to this rabble! But something about the way she'd said this, with such utter conviction and passion, made him take a new look at his own beliefs. He asked if he could come with Trish to the homeless shelter where she would be serving. He eventually became a regular volunteer and devoted many hours to this work. He said that at the shelter he met people whose life stories were not that different from his own. Some were addicts, and many were dysfunctional for other reasons, that was true. But Dean could no longer deny that, regardless of how far they had fallen, they were human beings just like him.

The experience of working with the homeless tore down barriers Dean admitted he did not even know were there. When he passed people begging in the streets, he now felt compassion for them. He felt that they were members of his tribe. Working at the kitchen he learned the truth of the old maxim, "to give is to receive." He learned to see beyond the filth and dysfunction that many homeless people display, to the human heart which was very much like his own. He also got in touch with his own fear of poverty, and that fear diminished the closer he allowed himself to get to the people he served.

Dean's experience is perhaps unusual. Not all of us are going to find the answers we seek by working in a soup kitchen. However, his story does illustrate how a change of perception can shift the way we relate to ourselves and the world around us. The walls he tore down not only allowed him to confront some of his own fears about living, they allowed him to experience himself in the context of sacred tribe.

Life lives through us. Everything we might encounter—moments of fun and pleasure, periods of crisis and acute challenge—all this and more rip away the old and render us changed. The French philosopher and essayist Henri Bergson once said, "That which we perceive as disorder may prove to be just an element of a higher order which for the moment we cannot see." The uncontrollable or unexpected can radically shift our ability to experience a new range of possibilities, joys, and successes that moments before seemed impossible.

Although these breakthrough moments can seem extraordinary, the fact is we are constantly encountering them. Sometimes we recognize the gift, sometimes we don't. If we live separately, with the perspective that we are always in competition with others, this level of sharing, and the richness of experience that goes with it, eludes us. We all end up scrapping with others for each morsel instead of sharing our riches with the tribe, and thus strengthening us all.

As long as we perceive ourselves as alone, we keep our lives secret, hide the road maps to our successes, hide our failures behind shame. Not only do we hide these secrets from others, we hide them from ourselves, limiting our understanding of the strengths and inner resources that are available to us. When we have those simple moments of tribal sharing, we are moved and delighted. We know the value of sharing each and every day. Then, living tribally, we have new values.

Our strengths and our lessons become valued assets, not in a selfish way, but as part of the abundance of the tribe. We recognize that the whole tribe benefits by everyone in the tribe being seen, valued, taught, cared for, loved and strengthened. Sharing and generosity become highly valued commodities. In short, we begin to see that our greatest strength as a society is realized not by hoarding our personal gifts, talents, and experiences, but by bringing these to the community. We get back much more than we give.

One of our dear friends, a special effects producer, had just wrapped up a job on a major motion picture. A group of us went with him to see the film opening in San Francisco. Sitting beside him, waiting for the film to begin, we asked, "Why are you so much more excited about this film than any other you have made?" He replied, "I decided when we began this film that not only were the special effects going to be better than they had ever been before, but that I wanted the making of the film to be a wonderful tribal process for the effects artists. For months as I drove to work I would ask myself, 'How can I build a supportive, creative, community today?'"

He went on to say that, in all the years of his career, never had he experienced such good feelings following the wrap of a film. He said that he received countless messages and phone calls from crew members, saying that working on this film had been the most rewarding experience of their careers. He had not told a single person that he was instilling sacred tribal values into the film making process. But there was abundant feedback from the people who worked with him that his efforts had been fruitful indeed.

FINDING OUR TRIBAL ROOTS

Through the kinds of tribal practices we'll be working with in this book, we create maps for living. We give and get validation for life's experiences. We receive permission to risk, to fail, to succeed. We begin to receive support where there has been none, to have mentorship in the areas where we don't have formal education. We gain courage in the places where, instead of the willingness to try, we have demanded of ourselves that we know. And how can we know... if we make it up for ourselves, try and fail, try again, all sequestered in the darkness of our own individual experience? Life needs to be lived out in the open for all to see, take heart from, and learn by. We all gain strength in this way, drawing from the wealth of wisdom gathered through the experiences of tribal consciousness.

We touch the roots of our tribal strengths and connections each day of our lives. But if we are to have the full benefit and comfort of these links with each other, we need to practice, to find those little templates that allow us to make the important transition from seeing to full recognition. Only then can we embrace the field of common human experience that bonds us all as one.

Voices of the Tribe

I started the year not really feeling anything. Hiding behind my job and other responsibilities, I did not realize that I was actually feeling empty. But, as I was surrounded by others, I experienced what it was like being part of a tribe, part of something bigger, caring about others.

I am constantly feeling surprised about how each day, both professionally as well as personally, I am now approaching life so differently, taking risks, and discovering how much I am really capable of being....
—Marcus Jung

This tribe started me on a journey into my own soul, discovering areas I was completely unfamiliar with. Opening one door led to many others... and this journey is still magnificently unfolding.
—Kitt Goldberg

PART

II

_____

THE SEVEN SACRED

TRIBAL VALUES

INTRODUCTION

A number of years ago Carole and I (Jodi) were sitting in a circle in Bali with a group of Westerners and Anom, a master mask maker. I found myself curious about how he had learned to carve such exquisite masks. I asked him to describe the process to us, and this is the story he told us:

ONE DAY, as a young boy, I went to my father who was a mask maker. I told him I wanted to begin carving masks. I couldn't wait to have my own knife, and to feel the sleek mahogany wood in my hand. My father said he would teach me, and immediately sent me off to study the sacred Hindu stories of the Ramayana and the Mahabharata. I understood what was expected of me, and didn't return to him until I knew those stories by heart. Four years later, I approached my father once again, ready to begin my lessons of carving the wood, and this time he sent me to learn to play the gamelan. The gamelan is a most important instrument of the Balinese orchestra, for it is played during the mask dances. One fine day I returned, now a dancer, a musician and story teller, and my father handed me a carving knife and a block of wood. And so I began. I could never have become a mask maker simply by cutting the wood. The masks might have taken their proper shapes, but they would never have been imbued with the vitality and the spirit they needed to hold. I had to know the masks in my body, in my voice, in their sound and in their spirit. And today, when I carve the masks, I become the mask's dance and story, and the mask comes alive.

As I listened to Anom's story, I remembered hearing Marilyn Kind, an athlete on the U.S. Olympic team from 1972 to 1976 saying, "Olympians are ordinary people... ordinary people who have accomplished extraordinary things..." Anom didn't become one of the finest mask makers in Indonesia simply by hoping for it. It took more than ten years of his life before he even had a piece of wood and a knife in his hands. He had to start with an intention, and then he had to take action. He had to practice living the values he wanted to embrace. His discipline and commitment made that possible.

Our longing for sacred tribal connection can only be fulfilled if we are willing to begin a daily practice of the values that create tribal reality. Whether you live in a village in Thailand or the Serengeti plains, whether you are hoping to enrich your own nuclear family, your workplace, or the community where you live, sacred tribal values are universal. When these values are linked to everyday action, a rich livingness fills our ordinary world in a most extraordinary way.

As you explore the sacred values which we'll be describing in the following chapters, remember that you already experience many rich moments of living this way. The practices we describe here will help you begin to live such moments *on purpose*. All you need is desire and the willingness to act. Begin somewhere, however small and simple it may seem. The important thing is beginning!

Start with any tribe. A tribe may be just two, as in any intimate relationship. Or it can be a work group, a family, a community of friends. It can even be only yourself, with a new set of perspectives about your relationships with the people around you, and how you relate to yourself.

Keep in mind that some of the biggest changes in our lives have begun with small movements of thought, feelings, and ideas. This can mean just paying more attention than usual when you have interactions with other people.

Each time you practice these values—by telling a story, or offering mentorship, or expressing appreciation for another person—a huge difference is made. Pay attention to these differences. Recognize what has occurred. Notice the changing patterns of your life as the fabric of tribe gets woven through these new kinds of interactions.

Be willing to try new things.

Have the courage to begin, letting your heart and your desire lead your actions.

Be willing to fail and stay in good humor, accepting that everything won't always work out as you planned.

Tell people that you want to create tribe with them. Enlist their help. You'll probably discover, as we have, that the word "tribe" is important to people. It stimulates their creativity and imagination.

Start using the word tribe in everyday conversation. It's contagious. People will want to hear more about what it is, what it means to live in tribe.

Be patient. Nurture your tribal garden with the excitement and love you've already begun to discover in this new undertaking.

Incorporate the ideas in this book into your daily practice. Get up each day and ask yourself, "How can I put one of these values into practice today?" As you move forward with your tribal practices, bear in mind that you are involved in an organic growth process. Tribe is like any living organism—it must grow at its own speed and strengthen in its own time. Only then can we start enjoying its rich benefits.

We have a friend who once visited the retreat community of Findhorn. Linda was a real go-getter, busy all the time, never resting. After she had been at Findhorn for a week, she went to one of the farm managers and said, "It seems to me that you run this place rather inefficiently. The community gets up, has tea, meditates, works a little, takes a break, works a bit more, rests, has lunch, plays or naps, meditates, and then works a bit more. You'd get much more done if the community members would devote more of their time to working the gardens. Then everything would grow better and faster."

The manager studied Linda's face for a moment, drew a deep, luxurious breath, and then relaxed back in his chair. After a moment, he replied, "Gardens grow the same way a soul does. You plant them, nourish them, and you wait patiently. And in time they bear fruit." He encouraged Linda to spend her time at Findhorn in soul time, seeing what would take root in her own soul if she let herself be with it, growing as a garden grows.

Let your communities grow this same way. Like the ancient image of the silk scarf being drawn across the granite mountain, with trust, patience, and time the mountain gives way to the scarf. Similarly, our separate, dismembered lives give way to sacred tribe. Remember Anom, who set out to become a master mask maker, and through the process became an extraordinary dancer and musician. The process of creating tribe in your life will develop aspects of yourself that you may have only dreamed were there! Perhaps you will become a wonderful mentor, a storyteller, a ritual maker, or be of service in countless other ways.

As you begin, it's difficult to predict where your journey will take you. We know, from first hand experience, that a new model of tribe is possible. It doesn't happen by accident, by simply saying we want it, or by hoping that someday, if we believe in it, pray for it, and long for it, we will have it. It starts in simple ways, with simple actions. It starts with you, and with me, with everyone who hears the word tribe and feels called to bring these values into their life.

When we say the word tribe, it should no longer bring up images of a Utopian, regressive, innocent tribe in the wilderness, a tribe with no dissension, struggle, or strife. Rather, the tribe of which we speak comes from a shift of consciousness, a new way of looking at and experiencing our lives. Just as an orchestra needs many sounds, and notes from low to high, the tribe must also carry richness and diversity. If that richness and diversity can be seen and celebrated, then each tribe member can be integrated into our own hearts and lives. Sometimes this is difficult. But even the parts of ourselves that we struggle with are necessary to the tribe. Tribes with no dissension or strife die out, for within them there is not the diversity that makes it possible for life to prevail.

MOVING AHEAD

The following chapters discuss the sacred tribal values and give you ways to begin practicing them. You can use them in sequence or randomly. You can decide which one is most compelling and most appropriate for the situation you wish to create. We encourage you to target one area, one group of people with whom you want to create conscious tribe. That's the place to begin. We suggest that you gather a small group together, if possible, and begin these practices there.

The seven values you'll find in this section describe the building blocks of sacred tribe. You can use them in your families, communities, offices, marriages, and with yourself. We have been exploring these values and living them consciously for years. And now, from our tribe to yours, we invite you to join us in creating living sacred tribes everywhere!

3

THE FIRST VALUE: BELONGING

This we know: All things are connected like blood which
unites one family. All things are connected.

—*Chief Seattle, 1854*

Out beyond ideas of wrongdoing and rightdoing,
there is a field. I'll meet you there.

When the soul lies down in that grass,
the world is too full to talk about.
Ideas, language, even the phrase each other
doesn't make any sense.

—*Rumi*

D O I BELONG? In modern life we consciously or unconsciously ask ourselves this question many times every day.
When I am standing in line at the supermarket and the little child in his mother's arms ahead of me looks at me and smiles,
do I dare smile back? Do I talk to the child or mother? Is there any
way in the world that I belong with this mother and child, enough
to acknowledge the child's friendliness? Or would I be perceived as
an intruder, a threat? At work, when I am transferred to a new de-
partment, at what point can I say, "I belong"? If I marry and am at
the gathering of my spouse's family, might I be in error to assert my
belonging too soon? What can I call my community? My neighborhood?

The Hmong people don't question whether or not they belong. They just do! Their daily experience and their enactment of simple ritual constantly mirrors back to them their connections with the land, with people of all ages, and with their tasks within the tribe. They belong to their families within the tribe, to the growing cycles, to the moon, and to the sunrise and sunset. They belong because they live their lives in ways that link them to humanity, to life, to the invisible forces of the universe, and to themselves. And since it is clear to them that they belong, they act like it!

In modern life we have created lifestyles of separation, forgetting the spiritual bonds we have with each other—bonds that transcend property lines and privacy. This separation makes it difficult for us to feel we're tribe members of our companies, families, communities, and of the earth. We need to know ourselves as members of the global tribe.

BELONGING

Something deep in my soul guided me to summer camp. I (Carole) had longed to be part of something larger than myself. It was at camp that I had my most powerful experiences of connection to tribe and to spirit. I began to experience how our spiritual essence is linked with tribe.

My life changed on a Sunday morning. I was sitting in my temple's Sunday school classroom when a woman representing a Jewish summer camp presented a slide show. I cannot say what happened but I was transfixed. I knew, without a doubt, that I had to go her camp. It was an epiphany, with a door to a new world. I knew that I had to walk through that door. I went home and begged my parents to send me for the whole six week summer session. It was an overnight camp, and I wouldn't even be eligible to go for three weeks, much less six, until the following summer. I was only six years old.

I begged and begged. Something in my tone convinced my parents to go to bat for me. They did. Somehow they convinced the temple that I would be okay there, just as I had convinced them. And they enrolled me for the entire six weeks. I was not about to be denied!

The Sabbath rituals held a particular magic for me. All week long we were normal campers, our days filled with archery, swimming, arts and crafts. But on Fridays we stopped all activities and prepared for the Sabbath. We would rest, sit, tell stories, be together. And we would bathe, take out our ritual white clothes, and as the day gave way to sunset, we would stand on the front steps of our cabin, dressed in our best whites, and wait for the procession to reach us. It would start way off at the top of the meadow. The rabbi would lead, blowing his horn in a call to prayer. Behind him would be the camp elders, then the musicians with their guitars, followed by the drums, all singing the age-old songs of redemption and grace.

The procession would first go to the boys' side of the camp, where each cabin of children, from the oldest to youngest, would fall into this line, becoming one voice, one intention. We could hear them as they came down through the forest and across the bridge over the stream. They came into the girls' camp, again gathering each cabin of children from oldest to youngest, until, finally, my cabin joined. I was the youngest girl in the camp that first summer, and so I was the last in this magnificent line. I felt as if I had been picked up and was being carried by a divine thread. I felt whole. I felt part of something magnificent.

Singing, we walked to the dining hall, which had been transformed for this ritual. The dingy, beat-up round wooden tables had been draped with white cloths. A pair of Sabbath candles in silver candlesticks sat on each, with a loaf of braided bread and a small cup of wine. We stood in our whites, bringing our voices together, singing prayers in Hebrew, prayers I had never heard before, in a language I could not understand. But my heart could understand the joy of standing as one, one prayer, one voice, one song. All week long we had been campers, engaged in the usual day to day activities. We laughed and played, fought and made up. But tonight was different. Tonight we were joined together in something magnificent. Tonight we were linked through what was the highest in each of us. We sat at dinner and our very conversation somehow reflected the grace of the moment. We were gentle with one another, and generous. We loved each other a little more unconditionally. After dinner, after the prayers were sung, we spent hours clapping and singing in joyous celebration.

The next day, Saturday, each cabin took its turn leading the Sabbath service. No matter what the age of the children, each had their turn to write and lead the prayers and the sermon. And this is how it was every Sabbath for the whole summer.

I came back to this camp every summer for nine years. And every year I moved up a bit in the line, bringing more capacity and more understanding to the services I helped write and lead. As the years passed, the Hebrew words that had once been so strange and foreign to my ears became songs of praise that filled my heart, my whole being. Every year upon my return to this camp, my feelings of belonging were renewed.

What happened each summer was my initiation into the magic of tribe. We were more than individual campers, individual personalities. We were a tribe. The feelings of belonging, of being part of the whole, came automatically. As camp came to an end each season, I grieved the loss. I mourned the loss of knowing, so absolutely, that I was part of something that mattered deeply, and the loss of contributing to that which I loved.

CHOOSING SEPARATION OR BELONGING

How, in our isolation and separation, do we reclaim a sense of belonging? We have learned to place a high value on independence, and we may fear becoming dependent. If you and I belong to each other then we're linked—we need each other. We must both be aware of each other, and even more frightening, responsible for how we affect each other. Your decisions, your words, your actions will affect me, and I must realize that I'll have the same impact on you. We will both have to stay open and be willing to feel, not only our own feelings, but the feelings our actions bring up in each other.

If I perceive I am alone and separate, I can be free of all such complications and entanglements. Of course, I have also lost my connection, and any sense of my belonging. I may feel desperately lonely and detached, not only from humanity, but from life itself. We want to be individuals—but how do we hold on to our individuality and still enjoy a sense of connection?

To have both freedom and connection, we must consciously choose to practice actions that create belonging.

The link that is made when we say "us" is a powerful one. This link can be with another person, a family, a partnership, a company, or with the earth herself. Our consciousness of belonging, of being a part of, is basic to our health and well being. This doesn't mean that we must sacrifice our sense of self. On the contrary, we truly become us only when we bring all that we are as individuals to our partnership.

Let's look at a group of businessmen practicing tribal belonging:

A group of executives dressed in blue jeans, sweat shirts, and sneakers stands in a circle, listening to the wind, looking up at the majestic redwood trees, reflecting on the day. Some are so moved they have tears in their eyes. Others feel inspired, filled with strength and capacity that they hadn't known for a long time. The instructors remind them of what they had practiced that day, and ask each of them what they want to put into practice when they go back to the office.

Billy, a project manager, recalls his first experience that morning at the ropes course, when he let himself fall backwards, be caught by his colleagues, and then lowered gently back to the ground. "I've always known how to rely on myself to get things done, but haven't trusted others. I'm realizing that I can accomplish so much more when I ask for help and let people support me. People have an easier time relating to me when I speak about what I actually can and can't do, and let others excel at things I'm not good at. Everybody's win was my win today."

Another person, who had come to the day worried about his fear of heights, tells how he had actually climbed thirty feet up a tree as others held a belay line for him, cheering him on. He says at times it seemed they were taking each step with him, supporting him in some invisible way he did not understand.

Jean remembers her personal triumph that afternoon. That morning she had sworn to herself that she would never allow her feet to leave terra firma. So naturally she hadn't wanted to attempt the high ropes event, climbing up to a height of 30 feet! The group encouraged her, and when she successfully completed the event, she saw the inspiration in her co-workers' eyes, felt their support in her heart, and swelled with pride at her accomplishment.

"The greatest part was that when I started climbing the tree I already knew that I was going to fail, but I still wanted to try, and maybe even reach the goal of crossing the log thirty feet up. I was certain that if I reached the top, my knees would buckle. I had to accomplish the task by myself, but when I started to climb and yelled, 'Holy Kamoly!' to relieve my stress, from below me I heard my teammates yelling cheers, and actions I could take to succeed. This whole experience has changed my outlook. Now I know that when I begin a project, I can call on others within my company for assistance. Working together, I know we can achieve more than I thought I could."

Sally remembers how she felt when they successfully got the whole group over a fifteen foot wall, with no ladder or ropes.

"During the course, I saw a spectacular display of teamwork. There were no boundaries, competition, separate departments. Everyone was drawing from each other's energy. The exchanging of ideas, trials, errors, and successes were shared together as one. We laughed so much! I suddenly realized that I have never seen a team before today, only groups of people performing tasks side by side."

I, Me, Mine Versus Us, We, Our

Sadly, so many of us can make the same statement about our most intimate friendships, our families, our communities, even our marriages. We've lost our tribal vocabulary, and with it the behaviors that create the magic that occurs when any group of people gathers with the desire and willingness to become an "us." We are individuals, and that individuality is important. But that individuality is truly experienced when we bring it into service to something larger than ourselves—when we bring it into the service of an "us."

We'd do well to remind ourselves that human life is tens of thousands of years old, yet the highly personalized way of life that most of us take for granted today has existed for only about 300 years. Prior to the reign of individualism, village life and tribal ways characterized most of human existence. There was an ingrained understanding that the health and the strength of each individual member depended on the health and strength of the whole, the tribe; likewise, the well-being of the tribe was dependent on each person within it being a healthy and strong contributor. Belonging isn't simply an individual urge; it is a universal drive that is essential to the cosmic order itself.

We have so much to learn from Nature about the powers of tribe. Sit and watch ants at work. Each one moves independently, but as they pass one another they reach out their antennae and touch, acutely aware of the others, of those who have gone before, and those who are coming after. It is so easy, when we are not working in the context of us, to forget that we have an impact on everyone around us, and that we are part of everything.

Imagine being in the Hmong village for a moment. Life is going on around you in an endless swirl. The people you see must pool their resources to survive. Requests for help are taking place throughout the day. There is no expectation that any of us could do life on our own. What you see all around you is a Möbius strip of interdependence: the medicine man needs the hunter to gather food, the women can't give birth without the midwife. You see older men and women's roles shifting within the tribe as they age, with an unspoken recognition that each and every individual, regardless of ability, is necessary to the whole, to the alchemy of the tribe. At the center of it all is that feeling we call belonging.

Everyone and everything is interdependent in this village. What a relief! Who we are is enough! In the context of a real, working tribe, we feel adequate, because we are. We have a place. We belong. We don't have to wonder if we are part of something—our very presence and participation is integral to an invisible fabric that makes all that is going on around us strong and satisfying.

Here, we would never expect everyone in the village to be a medicine man, hunter, and midwife. But individuals would emerge from within the tribe to serve in each of these ways. It would be unnecessary to duplicate efforts, to compete for whose idea is the best. We could get on with bringing our full energy and attention to the things we feel passionate about.

What we are talking about here is not merely a change in behavior but a shift in consciousness, from being an "I," standing alone, to being a "we," standing together. This is the shift from an individual consciousness to a tribal consciousness.

FIRST WE HAVE TO CARE

Caring is easy—when we care. That sounds like a trick statement but there is actually a great deal of wisdom in it. Most people report there is a direct relationship between their personal satisfaction in something they are doing and how much they care or believe in the project. During times when we can't remember why our jobs matter, or when we roll over in the morning and look at our partners and think, "Are you still here?!," or when our community projects are taking too much time, effort, and money, or when our family life has settled into a rut of mediocrity, these are the times when the practice of caring is essential—and when it becomes a challenge.

Caring is risky. What if we care and the other doesn't? What if we care less than the other? What if we care and we are judged for it? What if we care and we fail? If we don't address these what ifs, we will continue to be isolated, lonely, and limited in our endeavors.

Caring means we have to endure being vulnerable to rejection, vulnerable to failure, vulnerable even to success. One of our favorite things to do with a group is to have them all get up and walk around the room, mingling with each other, telling of their fears of being rejected. They walk around the room saying things like, "I feel so awkward!" "Nobody will like me." "They'll think my idea is stupid." "Nobody wants to hear what I have to say." After the group has done this for a while, we stop them and pose the question, "Since everyone is walking around saying these things to themselves, fearing rejection, have you ever wondered who is available to do the rejecting?"

WHO IS AVAILABLE TO DO THE REJECTING?

One night many years ago I (Carole) was invited by my friend Stuart, a screenwriter, to have dinner with him and his friends.

Given that his friends were famous movie stars, I was nervous. I spent the day picking out the right outfit, getting my hair and nails done, concerned about what I would say to them, what they would think of me.

As the hour of our meeting approached, my friend Stuart picked me up at my hotel. From the moment I got into his car to the moment we arrived at the restaurant, I questioned, "But what will they think of me? What will I talk to them about? What if I stare?" As my anxiety built, I finally blurted out, "Did you tell them anything about me? What do they know?"

Stuart's reply was, "Well, they did ask me what you do for a living."

"And?" I babbled. "And? Don't leave me hanging!"

Stuart glanced in my direction, paused, then replied: "When I told them what you do for a living they said, 'Oh no, she's a workshop facilitator! What will she think of us? What will we say to her? What will we talk to her about?'"

I burst out laughing. It had never occurred to me that persons of fame and stature would be just as intimidated by me as I was of them. When we arrived at the restaurant Stuart shared our conversation with the others, and suddenly we were just four people, sitting at a table enjoying ourselves.

In my experience most of us do care, do want to belong. But we know so little about what to do to satisfy those desires. In the midst of our fear of rejection, we need to be willing to risk loving and being loved, trying and failing. We must also risk listening to and telling the truth, and be willing to care and offer our caring into the tribe.

When we make the shift from me and mine to us and our, we start to feel the desire to bring what is best in each of us to the tribe.

A few years ago, during halftime at a Los Angeles Lakers basketball game, there was a ceremony for Magic Johnson's retirement. Magic came to the microphone and gave a moving speech about how much he was going to miss being "one of the boys." Along with his teammates, he especially thanked Larry Bird, his opponent on the Boston Celtics, for being such an incredible ball player. Being in competition with Larry caused Magic to bring out the best in himself. He said that, without Larry, there could be no Magic. He went on to talk about how his association with this group had not only developed his skills as a ball player, but had grown him up into being a man.

Most of us aren't different from Magic Johnson in this regard. We need a reason to be magnificent, to bring out our best, to stand with others who are doing the same. Without a tribal consciousness, we can end up being great alone, excelling, accomplishing—all while getting more and more lonely. When we show up at our jobs, or anywhere else in our lives, acting as members of a tribe that cares about what we create, we honor ourselves and each other. This kind of experience is profoundly fulfilling.

We have to take on the simple practices of caring, of shifting from "me and mine" to "us and our." We have to feel our desire and our longing. Only then can we experience the magic of belonging to sacred tribe.

CAN ANYBODY SEE ME?

Over the years, hundreds of people have shared their own journal writings with us, communicating their experiences in our workshops. The themes we find mirrored back to us confirm what we have come to know about the tribal experience. The following journal entry was generously offered by a woman who felt that her story might help others grasp the value of taking the risk to be seen and heard.

I KNOW THAT THIS weekend in the workshop I must go public with my pain. It is my only hope for salvation from my internal prison... my only hope of beginning to communicate with my children who will be there, along with my husband whom I have not spoken with much at all during our five years of marriage: two souls locked away from each other.

Speaking in front of a large group is no issue for me—it's what I do for a living. What is so threatening is exposing my vulnerability, my incompetence, my less-than-perfect me. I am overcome with concern about exposing myself in front of my husband and my children, as almost involuntarily I feel my own hand going up, volunteering.

I don't remember how Jodi guided me toward self-exposure. We traveled deeply—I was a raw wound, seeping fear and pain in the presence of all these witnesses, especially my children. I remember speaking about being a good and accomplished child, whose father loved her for what she could do. Visibly trembling, Jodi asked me to climb in and access my vulnerability. Where did I withhold myself, offering a facade? If I let others see who I really am, what would they see?

"Please see my fear about really having you know me," I heard myself begin. Jodi asked me who was in the room that I most wanted to say these things to.

"My children," I said, without hesitation. And so they were there, looking deeply into my eyes, without cringing at the sight of their strong mother with tears streaming down her cheeks. I can't remember a deeper feeling of love and connection as when I told my son, "I want you to see my gratitude for having the courage to bring us together so we could know each other more fully. See my pride as you grow into a beautiful man."

And then to my daughter I said, "See my regret for the standards I've given you to live up to."

My heart broke as she began to cry. I looked into her eyes and said, "See my love and respect for you." Her tears of pain dissolved into love and relief, a beaming smile.

Others in the community joined us. They were right there with us. I felt so connected to them and to my family. This experience was so freeing. I felt so much strength in my openness and vulnerability, and I felt incredibly supported and loved by my children. I knew this was the beginning of a new relationship, a real relationship between us, based on the truth of who I am.

We must take the risk to express ourselves more fully in our lives if we want to experience belonging. We can't just wait to feel comfortable, loved or secure before we express ourselves. As we courageously reach out in our lives, like the Hmong people, we begin to feel that we belong. Because we do!

WE BELONG TO TRIBE, AND THE TRIBE BELONGS TO LIFE

In Bali, when a baby cries at night it is taken from its bed and held up to the night sky, as if to say, "Yes, you are suffering, but even in your suffering look up! See that you belong to God... to life." We all do indeed belong to life, and tribe is our link to our remembrance.

When we know and remember that we do belong and always have, when we experience that we are one of the threads of a fabric intricately woven into a thing of beauty, then we can experience each moment and every thread of our lives the same way.

A WEEKEND OF REVELATION

The following is an example of such moments of belonging we witnessed during one of our gatherings:

As the weekend approached, a letter arrived announcing what the group should bring: pictures, mementos, special objects, symbols of anything that represented important life events and experiences. The letter said to bring items from all aspects of your life, from infancy through the present time.

The group gathered on the first evening and set out their altars of objects and photos. These extended all the way around the room, with themes ranging from childhood through death. The childhood altars were overflowing with baby pictures and toys, and were followed by adolescent altars, with motorcycle helmets, phonograph records, prom pictures, t-shirts, trinkets symbolizing that stage. The early adult altars were strewn with college and wedding pictures, love letters, jewelry. Next were the prime adult altars, filled with business cards, professional credentials, pictures of families, second marriages, mementos of loss including divorce and parents' deaths, objects symbolizing hobbies, exotic places visited. There were elder altars, with pictures of grandchildren, awards won, photos of bodies that had changed. Finally there were the senex altars, with symbols of retirement, new creative expressions, travels, grand parenting artifacts, a withering flower, a picture of a redwood tree.

On the last morning, a fifty-six-year-old internationally known author and business consultant sat in the circle with men and woman of all ages, sharing his experience of being with the altars all weekend. He wept as he told this story:

"I took the little boy that I once was by the hand and walked him through my life, showing him the man he had become. I showed him the man he had grown to be. I introduced him to my children, and felt how proud of my life I am. For a moment I remembered the pain of my childhood—what it had meant to me to be labeled 'learning disabled,' a disappointment to my family. I remembered the determination I felt as a child—to be someone, no matter what, to show everyone I could do something worthwhile. I could see the fruits of all that determination, remembered all the times I wanted to give up, could see how much I have achieved."

Then a woman in her early forties talked of feeling hope that her divorce might be leading her in a positive new direction. One of the men in the circle, who had a teenager who was having trouble in school, began to wonder if his son was perhaps going through exactly what he needed to. He dared to imagine that these troubles were not due to his lack of ability as a father, but to the necessary breaking away that teenagers must undergo. A young woman in her twenties felt the excitement of where her career might be leading her, and the gentleman in his sixties simply nodded knowingly.

Within the circle of these altars, and the sharing of this tribe, each of the individuals could begin to see and experience that they somehow belonged to their lives, and that their lives belonged to a much larger mystery. Their past challenges and pain made a little more sense.

The people who participated in this weekend took a great risk by sharing these stories from lives. By revealing so much of themselves to the group, they took a giant step into the practice of belonging. And from this belonging, they began to feel that their lives made sense. They were no longer alone. The artifacts and the stories of their lives were interwoven into a tapestry that revealed how, indeed, they were of one tribe, the tribe of humanity.

WHO TAKES THE FIRST STEP?

One of my (Jodi) favorite moments of belonging occurred during a pilgrimage I made to the Old City of Jerusalem. It was a Wednesday morning, the morning they do bar mitzvahs at the wall in the Jewish Quarter. Before I reached the wall I could hear the beautiful chanting as people gathered in prayer and celebration. Their bodies swayed from side to side, their heads bowed and covered as they spoke the ancient words of the Torah. This was all happening in an environment of commotion, with several services happening simultaneously.

I walked a short distance to the Christian quarter to visit the site where it is believed that Christ was crucified. From far away I saw people lighting candles and bowing their heads, singing their prayers of thanksgiving.

Then I walked ten minutes further to the Moslem quarter, and stood in awe of The Dome of the Rock, and was drawn to the voices singing within the mosque. I removed my shoes and walked in. I saw heads covered, bodies rocking in prayer, lighting candles and uttering words of devotion. All I could feel that morning was how much the same thing was happening all over Jerusalem each day, even if these sometimes warring tribes couldn't see it. I could feel myself as part of a wave of people who loved the sacred, who practiced devotion, and who loved life. I knew that I belonged to all of the places of worship I had visited that morning, and more than that, we all belonged to each other and to life.

The memory of what I witnessed that day has become a constant touchstone for me, reminding me that we do already belong. Even in my loneliest moments it tells me that life hasn't forsaken me; it is simply waiting for me to remember.

When Anom, the Balinese mask maker, makes his masks, eventually someone comes from a village and buys one. The Balinese honor their spirits just as they would honor anything or anyone in life—they make no distinctions between human and non-human forms. So when the new mask, which represents a spirit, is brought into the village, a great ceremony is performed, welcoming the mask, its magic, its presence and its purpose. Food is cooked and offerings of delicious sweets and fruits are brought. These are placed below the altar that holds the mask. When the villagers feel that the deities within the mask have had their fill, the food is then given to each family in the village. And every day after that, someone from the village brings a small offering of food to the mask, paying homage to the spirit it represents. The mask is cared for in the same way we would care for a beloved friend.

We could care for the people in our lives in the same beloved way. Someone has to go first. Someone has to say, "There is an us. I remember, and I will take the steps to create and take care of it." Anyone can begin the practice of belonging at any moment of their lives. It takes only a moment of silence, of touching the sacred, to say the words, "I belong."

Voices Of The Tribe

The Mud Ritual

So tender I was and vulnerable,
as I shed my skin,
slowly, with the slight hesitation of my new found tender shyness
like a newborn must feel when he enters the world.
Then, to find my rhythm with the clan
and the great planetary soul, and the great sky father
racing through me the energies of both
feeling this tribal dance and ritual move through me
flowing like a lost soul living a new life.
Forgiveness of my past present and future
hearing the cries of my tribe,
hearing the voices resonate in my ears...
like gifts unto their own.
The joy of life
how fresh and clear and calm I feel,
connecting to everything and everyone.
I pray to live my life in union with my beating heart
and the hearts of my tribe.

Let me not forget... and...
Let me remember.

—Diana Everline

As we sit in the circles for a while
we make soup in the middle.
We pour ourselves in.
We bring many different stories,
reveal our fears and our secrets,
offer art that comes from our souls.
Laughing and crying and listening and dancing
we create the savor that only we can.
After passing ladles of honor and appreciation
we return home filled.

—Virginia M. Fleming

4

THE SECOND VALUE: RECOGNITION

The real voyage of discovery consists not in seeking new landscapes but in having new eyes.

—*Marcel Proust*

Life is like a lamp-flame; it needs a little oil now and then.

—*Kashmiri folk saying*

To KNOW WITH any certainty that we belong, we have to be recognized, acknowledged, given some form of feedback that says to us, "Yes, you are valued here. I see your struggles, your accomplishments, your fears and your pain. I see who you are, what you have experienced in your life." This fundamental process not only serves to confirm to us that we belong to a society, a tribe; it's a form of acknowledgment that goes deeper, helping us to understand the ways we matter to others, and how we make a difference in their lives. Through recognition we learn about our impact on others, and theirs on us. We learn the ways in which we truly make a contribution to our tribe, and this understanding brings a deep feeling of worth.

"Watch me, Mommy!" How many parents have heard this cry a million times as their children are growing? One of the ways a child begins to know and understand himself is through the way people respond to him. I (Jodi) am especially struck by this when I take Carole's son, Zachary, to a park. He climbs on the play structures, shouting to me, "Jodi, watch me jump! Jodi, look how high I'm swinging! Jodi, watch me go down the slide!" Understanding his need for me to help him see and know himself, I say things like, "Boy, Zachary, look how high you're swinging! I can't believe that you can climb that high. What a great climber you are!" As I do this he beams with pride.

I can see recognition's same power when Zachary is upset or frustrated. Then my response is a little different: "You seem really frustrated trying to get that toy to work!" Or, "I bet you're disappointed that we have to leave the park now. You were having such a good time." But these statements of recognition are equally as important. I don't try to change his feelings or his experience. Instead, I give him a reflection of how he appears to me in the moment, to help him learn how to see and understand himself more clearly. In this way, I help him become aware of the invisible forces influencing him.

If the tribe can give a child this kind of recognition, he learns not just how his actions affect and are valued by others, but also how to provide these important acknowledgments for himself. Recognition within the tribe builds internal skills for every individual, allowing them to develop self-confidence, guide themselves through hard times, and acknowledge themselves for big and small achievements. The child who receives this recognition develops an inner witness for himself. He becomes capable of giving himself praise, encouragement, and feedback.

Ultimately, the skills the tribe helps a person build through recognition contribute to the strength of the tribe as a whole. The child grows into an adult who is aware of, and therefore more capable of offering, his own value.

If we are parents or teachers, we may understand a child's need for recognition, but overlook that we need the same thing as adults. Recognition is one of the most meaningful ways we communicate to ourselves and each other that our feelings, thoughts, and life experiences—both disasters and triumphs—are real and important. They are seen, witnessed, honored, respected. Recognition can take us out of our isolation or sense of victimization by reminding us "This feeling you are having, this experience you have to endure, this moment of celebration has been lived before. Here is proof that you are part of a larger sphere, the tribe we call humanity."

Through recognition, the tribe can help the individual heal by simply mirroring back to him what is, rather than denying something difficult, becoming caretaking, or minimizing the importance of a simple contribution. The message that gets communicated along with this type of reflection is, "You can handle this. I know it's painful, but hang in there." Or, "Your happiness is wonderful." Or, "Your accomplishments and gifts matter to us all. They're important. We value them."

WITNESSING

Witnessing is a special kind of recognition. It's recognition without judgment, listening without attempting to change a person's response to what they're experiencing. Being witnessed helps us begin to truly open to what's happening in our lives. Released from the fear of judgment or criticism, we can start to accept difficult experiences, ones where we might feel inadequate, helpless, ashamed, or hurt.

Sometimes the strength of the witness is the only thing that holds us in our struggle. But if we can start to open to them, these experiences which were once so painful we could only reject them can start to become our teachers. That is why they are sometimes called "sacred wounds," and why standing witness is a responsibility just as sacred.

As tribe members, we can never overestimate the power of even simple acts of witness—someone taking our hand, making eye contact, or just sitting with us.

In the Jewish tradition there is a wonderful ritual of recognition when someone dies. They "sit Shiva" for ten days after the death of a loved one, wearing black clothes and sitting on a hard wooden seat, while friends, family, and the community come to sit with the family of the deceased and honor their grief. Witnesses come to visit but do not try to change the fact that the death has occurred. Instead, they serve as the mirror to reflect the mourning process.

SIMPLE ACTS

Gestures of recognition in our daily lives can appear so subtle and spontaneous as to seem insignificant. Yet there are times, such as times of need or grief, when even a moment of recognition can make a tremendous difference, a difference we remember the rest of our lives. To renew our tribal connections, we have to learn to appreciate how powerful our simple acts of recognition can be, every day. Most of us don't walk through life asking ourselves, "How can I offer someone recognition today?," yet this can be a renewing and inspirational daily practice. The following story helps to illustrate just this point:

All my (Carole) life, my mother had been depressed and suicidal, but in my conversations with her over the past several months she seemed to be doing better. So it took me by surprise when my father called to say that she had taken an overdose of sleeping pills and was in the hospital. Her chances of pulling through were slim.

As I boarded the plane to return home, I was beside myself. I loved and needed my mother, and was terrified that she would die. I was only twenty years old. In all the years of seeing her suffer, I had never given up hope that she or modern technology would find a way for her to live differently. She had moments of balance and pleasure in life and I had trusted that those moments would someday expand. I had looked forward to a time when the two of us could share our lives more fully. But as I flew to Ohio, I knew the truth. I could feel that she was dying.

I was wrapped in a cocoon of horror and terror. I wanted to cry out to her, "How can you leave me? I need you!" At the age of twenty, I often felt, as young adults do, that I was immortal and omnipotent. But all that was changed. On the inside, I was just a little girl whose mother was dying, and I couldn't imagine getting through life without her.

For eleven days my mother lingered, the thin thread of her life maintained by a respirator. I sat with her, stroked her hair, talked to her, pleaded and bargained with God. For eleven days I had no idea if she could hear me. Could she think, or make sense of my words?

And then the day came when the doctor told us that she was irreparably brain-damaged, and it was time to consider taking her off life support. Without any discussion, I knew what our decision would be. I don't remember the words we exchanged at that moment, nor do I recall how the order to take her off life support was carried out. But I do remember desperately searching all through the hospital for a pair of scissors. All I could think of was that I needed to have a lock of my mother's hair. I needed something to hold on to, something I could touch and smell. I knew that my mother would eventually become a distant memory to me, and I could not bear to think of living without her touch, her arms. I felt that my own life was slipping away as hers approached its end.

No one in the hospital would give me scissors. I was frantic. Then one of the nurses, who I'd like to believe intuitively knew what I was seeking and why, recognized my desperation and gave me the scissors. She didn't ask me a thing, not even, "Why do you need these?" She simply looked me in the eye and handed me the scissors. In that moment I felt recognized. Someone else had been here, knew my needs and acknowledged my mission. The gesture of handing me the scissors and recognizing me with her eyes was all the ritual I needed. I felt connected with my human tribe.

I went to my mother's bedside and snipped off a lock of her hair. I held her hand, lay down next to her in the bed, shoving aside the tubes and other paraphernalia that would no longer be required. Only then could I allow the life support to be removed. I was barely aware of the hospital staff as they went about their work, shutting off the machines.

Where just moments before the room had been filled with the monotonous rhythm of the respirator, and the busy sounds of the staff caring for this person who could no longer care for herself, the room was now still, filled with the last silent moments of my mother's life, which seemed to be trickling away. I watched the face of this woman who I loved so much, and from whose body I had come, as she ceased to breathe. I felt as if I were breaking apart. Never again would there be arms that could hold me in the immensity of my grief. Awed by the final cessation of life in this body I had known so well, I walked from the room, feeling empty and lifeless. I had no idea where I was.

I don't know how long I wandered through the hospital before sitting down on a chair. I might have sat there for an eternity, for I felt I was without a home, without an identity. The nurse who had given me the scissors sat down beside me and touched me lightly on the hand to get my attention. Very quietly she said, "I know what it is to lose a mother. You feel as though you cannot go on living, but you will. You will not always feel like this."

Hearing her words, I began to weep. I felt, finally, that I could pour out my grief. That nurse didn't stay with me long, nor did she hold me until it was over. She sat with me for a moment, then left me with the words that I have held on to for many years. This woman remembered for an instant that she was not only doing a nursing job, but that she and I were members of a tribe. For a moment she mothered me while my own mother died, just as in a village one woman might nurse the baby of another. She alone, out of all the people there, recognized my grief, and through her recognition, she held the possibility of a new day for me, because she had already lived it. She knew. And in her knowing she reached across the ocean of my grief with an outstretched hand.

As I look back on this experience as an adult, I am reminded how small actions can make a big difference.

Recognition makes it possible for us to see and know ourselves more fully, and it also allows us to find ourselves as part of the tribe, part of life. This kind of recognition is filled with healing, both for the person who offered the recognition, and for the person who received it. If only one other person stands outside our lives and says, "Yes, I see you, and I know what you are going through," even that much recognition of our struggle can give us courage and hope. With this kind of support from our tribe, we can find the courage to stay open to life. We might even be led into new adventures and opportunities.

THE POWER OF TRIBAL REFLECTION

People often stand up in our workshops and say, "I thought I was the only one." They often believe they're the only ones going through what they're experiencing. As a result, they don't know where to turn when navigating new territory. This isn't so much a product of their shortcomings as the result of an educational process and social structure that isolates us all from life. Outside our families and our small circles of work and leisure activities, in today's world we're alone.

When a tribe is formed, people share their life experiences with others, others who until then may have felt alone and isolated, even alienated. As one person shares their story, others with them can slowly begin to see a new picture of their own lives emerging. Where the horizon had seemed barren, they can now see new possibilities, new paths through the wilderness into the unknown. Here are some examples that we have had the privilege to hear, and later share with others:

The retired doctor tearfully tells his story about his struggles to turn over his practice to his younger associates. Then his face lights up as he tells us about the sailing trip he just completed, and his plans to begin the garden he's dreamed of planting for years. As he tells his story, men in their thirties and forties are given a new perspective on aging. It brings up their own feelings about one day turning over the reins to a younger person, and they discuss this with animation. They see there is time to live dreams and to fulfill plans that their busy careers squeezed out of their younger lives.

A forty-five-year-old woman speaks of the joys of her second marriage, and people in the room who are newly separated or recently widowed suddenly breathe easier, aware that perhaps a fulfilling new relationship might still be possible. Dreams of romance in their lives are once again realities to them, affirmed by a member of their tribe.

A mother and her twenty-five-year-old daughter reflect on the challenging transitions they have made together in the last ten years, and two mothers of difficult teenagers begin to think that maybe their own daughters don't hate them after all. Perhaps they are just figuring out how to take control of their lives, to establish an identity separate from their parents. They see that their relationships with their children must change to provide room for the child to grow toward adulthood. The tribe mirrors back a continuum that no person alone could easily see.

The father of a sixteen-year-old girl reads a poem that expresses his regret that he hasn't known how to talk with her during the years she was growing into womanhood. His poetry tells how she feels like a stranger to him now. His love and his sense of helplessness are palpable. The women in the room are so moved they begin to discuss their own relationships with their fathers. Several of them tell the man that because of his poem they now know their own fathers more deeply. Every father in the room can feel this father's grief, a reflection of their shared experience.

A MINER AND HIS DAUGHTER

He was just a simple miner
Struggling to survive,
With a daughter nearing womanhood.
His wife had long since died.

Each day he dug a trail,
Put the iron in his cart,
Then home to see his daughter,
Who dug a trail to his heart.

Their shack was small and humble
On a lonely desert site;
His daily glass of whiskey
Helped to ease him through the night.

His daughter was about to change
Her body was aflame,
Like the desert burning through the day;
By night it's not the same.

Lately when he spoke to her,
Usually he found
Her lips were sealed, as tightly
As the iron in the ground.

The passage through to womanhood
For her was bittersweet;
How could he know to comfort her
When he found the bloodstained sheet.

Her mood was changing constantly.
It took him by surprise,
Like the shadows on the mountainside
That change before one's eyes.

He knew the beauty of her soul,
That part she could not hide;
Though cactus may be prickly,
There's softness deep inside.

His thoughts returned to younger days
When he wasn't getting flak,
When she was thrilled to see him,
And jumped into his lap.

He poured himself another drink
And downed it with a shove,
And hoped that soon she'd come to know
The depth of father love...

Slowly our poet begins to know that he is not alone. He discovers that his helplessness isn't a personal failure; rather, it's part of a father's job to bear the grief when his daughter moves into this new territory, that new stage of life that he cannot enter with her. He hears from the women in the room, once adolescent daughters themselves, and can imagine a future reconciliation with his daughter. He sees there is life beyond teenage parenting, a stage so difficult but so necessary.

As important as these moments of recognition are, they're all too rare in our culture. Usually we don't make room for such profound sharing, such essential moments of acknowledgment, nor do we appreciate their significance as part of our education.

When seen through tribal eyes, and thereby recognized, the events of ordinary life take on new depth and meaning. And only through these tribal eyes can we truly see our gifts and abilities, our failures and achievements, our victories and regrets, our joys and sorrows, and begin to know ourselves.

RECOGNITION VERSUS RESCUING

We are a "rescuing" society. We want to make it better, change it, make the hurt go away, stop bad things from happening. We can't. And more importantly, we shouldn't. Sometimes we realize that following our impulse to rescue, to make things better for a person in pain, might be the most destructive thing we can do.

I (Carole), recall working with one of my clients who was HIV-positive. She was a young woman, with wonderfully strong ties to her family. As the years went by, the family grappled with the woman's illness, and were quite successful. They grew closer. When the young woman's T-cell count dropped dramatically, she moved into her parents' home and the ties became even stronger. She developed many of the illnesses associated with HIV. The family came together, wanting to bring more healing into their family.

In one of our sessions, it became clear that the taboo subject for this family was death. They could not let themselves speak of it.

Instead, they focused on questions such as: "What can we do to make her well? What else do we need to do for each other?" This family had reached the limits of what they could do about the physical disease. Now it was time to begin the healing, and address their thoughts and feelings about the daughter's possible death.

Gently we opened the topic. This day, the family was able to tell the truth about their fears. The parents poured out their grief, their feelings of helplessness, how inconceivable it was to them that they would never hold their grandchild. The mother talked about how horrible it was to see her daughter sick and not be able to make her well. And the daughter talked about preparing to die. She talked about how much she felt she had to stay "up" so her family members wouldn't feel so bad.

The parents had been unable to voice their deepest feelings for fear of upsetting their daughter. The daughter had been afraid to upset her parents. Though they had struggled to avoid it, no one could change their painful truth. In the end, their desire to relieve the pain of the persons they loved was keeping them from the only thing that could. At last, through recognition, through witnessing, they removed the final barriers to their intimacy.

RECOGNITION HEALS
THE INDIVIDUAL AND THE TRIBE

Recognition is a tribal responsibility. We need to be seen and heard, and we need to offer this to each other. Through the process of recognition we have our emotional truths acknowledged and affirmed, and we're able to identify those who can teach and mentor us. Without the process of recognition, we don't know who lives in our village. We can't reap the benefits of our co-workers' talents, our neighbors' resources, our partners' and friends' life stories. We don't know who to call on when we need an understanding moment of tenderness, or a sympathetic ear.

What if we recognized each other consciously every day of our lives? What if we didn't have to feel so isolated and confused when we were grieving, or when we were sitting in the terrible feelings of failure? What if our accomplishments—moments when we had struggled and triumphed, worked hard and learned—were reflected back to us?

What if people knew what you had lived through, and sought you out for mentorship and wisdom?

One of the most profound examples of recognition I (Carole) have ever seen occurred in a workshop that I was teaching. A man, who I will call Jim, had in a moment of unguarded truth revealed that he had been in the Special Forces during the Vietnam War, and that he had killed many people. This revelation, while startling and difficult for the group to hear, was even more astonishing to Jim. He had never before spoken of his time in Vietnam. Since his return from the war he had simply tried to reintegrate himself into society, without looking back. When asked if he had been there, he would often say no.

Jim was wracked with guilt. He could barely look at the group as he said, "I've never been willing to talk about this. I've never told my wife, or children, my mother, not even many of my fellow vets, that I've killed so many people. I judge myself for it everyday, and I can't make any sense of it. Every day I have to live with the knowledge of the monster I am, hiding it from everyone I love. None of you could possibly understand if you weren't there. I have lived with this shame and guilt every day since I returned."

Jim stood in front of the group, having spoken the unspeakable. He looked out into a sea of faces, expecting to see their horror. As we let silence be Jim's witness, I asked the group if any of them live with something that they have spent a lifetime trying to make sense of, and come to terms with. Slowly, many hands began to rise. As if on some silent cue, each outstretched arm stayed in the air, the group trying to have Jim recognize that so many of them also had a monster that lives inside.

I invited Jim to consider that men who come back from war need to tell their stories, and in many cultures they do, in part to initiate the ones who weren't there. I asked him to consider that along with the guilt and shame, there must be something in him that could recognize the deepening and teaching that such an initiation must bring. There must be something gained, some capacity honed, that most people will never have. In some way his wound must be sacred. A glimmer of hope began to flicker in his eyes as he considered that, possibly, he might be redeemed from his horrible experience if it could contribute something.

While Jim's worst fear was that this revelation made him a monstrous outcast, I saw the group looking back at him with compassion and shared grief. Hands started to rise, as one by one the group began to offer Jim the kind of recognition that brings redemption. They began to tell him what they could learn or receive from a fellow tribesman who had walked the path that he had, and been initiated in such ways.

This is Jim's experience of it:

I LISTENED WITH disbelief as I heard people begin to speak. I was sure that I had just become an outcast. I opened my eyes and looked into the eyes of a man who seemed to be exactly my age. With teary eyes he said, "There but for the grace of God go I. You went, I didn't have to."

As I tried to believe that someone would ever say that to me, an older woman turned to me and said, "Without people like you, we wouldn't be safe."

Then a younger man looked at me with what even seemed like admiration and said, "Thank you for learning about courage. Thank you for giving up your innocence so I could keep mine. I don't know about facing death."

Another man reached his hand out and said, "Thank you for being willing to speak about this. I've killed, too, and your strength and wisdom helps me."

As I looked into the eyes of this tribe I saw faces filled with compassion and love, not the judgment and loathing I had expected. Then I noticed an Asian woman slowly beginning to rise out of her seat, her face a mask of grief.

"Jim, it means everything to me that you feel such shame and guilt. Those were my people that you killed, and in letting me see that it matters to you, I can begin to hate less, and love a bit more. Thank you."

In this moment, facing her and hearing the others, Jim began to feel the walls of twenty-eight years beginning to loosen their hold. He never would have imagined that he could be received in this way. This was the answer to the question, "Could it serve anyone to know?" We knew without a doubt when Jim said *"I now know that the war is really over."*

As the tribe offered recognition for Jim's terrible secret, his journey to healing began. He left the workshop and started to let those close to him know him more fully.

It wasn't only Jim who gained the benefit of this encounter. Each person who offered recognition had to somehow find compassion. By offering love without judgment, they could also face the parts of themselves that were hard to accept. Though they had to wrestle with their own fear, and the temptation to remain silent, as the tribe received Jim they delivered him to a path to self-acceptance. And in doing so, they affirmed their own.

We all need to receive this kind of recognition. But if we want to receive it, we all must make a practice of giving it first.

JUST AS WE ARE

Nietzche said that we must affirm our lives with "amor fati," the love of fate, the love of our destiny. If we do not carry the faith that even the most devastating experiences we live with serve a purpose, then the beauty and wholeness of our lives unravels from that one flawed thread. Recognition—the reflection back to us that our triumphs and failures hold a meaningful place in the tribe—helps us find the faith to embrace even the most overwhelming and difficult aspects of our lives.

Recognition of the kind we're describing here is healing and validating. It leads us to self-acceptance. With the offering and receiving of recognition we can begin to notice that every event in our lives, every part of us, even our "flaws" serve a meaningful purpose. And the possibility emerges that we can love ourselves and life just as we are.

Voices Of The Tribe

Anasazi Spirits

I am man
I am mountain
My peak reaches the heavens
and my roots pass through the ages of time
At my deepest
I bathe in the center of life
I have known many moons
and sustained many lives
Hearts have taken their first steps of mystery
yet more have heard the echo of the last sacred drum
I have been kissed by the rain—bitten by frost
stroked by the wind and burnt by the sun
oh—it feels so good to be alive
The night stars caress my soul and the moon cools my tender skin
My heart is full of the memories of man
who like the plants and trees were looking to grow
My heart is heavy from the thunder of migrating beast

who like man were just looking for food
My heart is beating to the silence of flight
from the bird of prey to the prey of bird
From here I can see the ends of the earth
and the depth in the blue of the sky
From here I witnessed your coming
as the rain washed the dust from my eyes
I am mountain
I am man
from here
I can go anywhere

—Jerry Fox

This is one woman's letter of recognition to her husband:

Dear Bob,

I married you, a strong man who loves and honors life. You are my teacher!

In the simplicity of your soul, you celebrate children and dogs and pumpkin pie, and stars and Klondike ice cream bars and tomato soup and music. And in the magnificence of your compassion you non-judgmentally embrace all of life, especially me. You allow me to tap your solid strength so I can honor the multi-faceted, unpredictable creative impulses of my soul.

I love you for who you are. After thirty-four years knowing so well who you are, I love you even more for who you shall become.

—Jan Smith

5

THE THIRD VALUE: RITES AND RITUALS

The function of ritual, as I understand it, is to give form to human life, not in the way of a mere surface arrangement, but in depth.

—*Joseph Campbell*

Initiation rites taken at the right time burn off what is no longer relevant, opening our eyes to new possibilities of our own uniqueness.

—*Carl Jung*

THE MOST COMMON rituals we enact in Western life include celebrating birthdays, graduations, or sacred holidays such as Hanukkah and Christmas. The rituals we enjoy around those special days remind us of their meaning and purpose. On the day of our birth we set candles on a cake for each year we have been on this planet. In lighting the candles and then blowing them out, we perform a ritual that symbolizes the years that are now behind us. From that day we go forward, born again out of the ashes of the years that have passed.

Tribes create rituals for life's passages, not only to bring the tribe together, but to illuminate a particular stage of life. For example, we all know that in order for birth to occur, some form of death must take place. At each stage of change we must say, "What is required of me at this time? What is appropriate for this passage?" Without ritualization, life can easily become a series of seemingly disjointed events, unrelated to any larger context. We need to enact rituals that highlight our initiations and transitions, honoring the changes, letting us know what is required at each stage, and how to develop in relationship to those requirements.

STANDING IN YOUR LIFE

AS WORKSHOP facilitators we were called into the circle to be part of the 'Stand if you...' exercise. On the surface, this is a simple ritual. A list of life events is read off to the group and people are asked to stand if that event is something they have experienced, or are experiencing in their lives right now. For example, the workshop conductor would say, "Stand if you are a parent."

Even now, my eyes fill with tears as I remember, with awe and respect, the mood of the group as we witnessed each other standing for our various initiations. Before our eyes we see the transformation of previously undervalued or even traumatic experiences into collective wisdom and healing from which we could all draw as a tribe.

I found myself standing in many, if not most categories. "Stand if you were ever married... divorced... had a child... sat with a dying person..." Tears now roll down my cheeks as I write this, the words on my computer screen pulling up these beautiful and painful memories of love and loss. All the disappointment, intimacy, and grief that I am still learning from my knowledge and beliefs about the value of life, family, and community come to life at this moment.

"Stand if your best friend died."

Oh, God, another unbearable loss! How can I let people see me so grief-stricken? I want to lay down on the floor and sob. It's not that I haven't processed this before, but somehow the ritual of standing to be seen as I am immersed in the feeling touches me deeply. I've been holding this all my life. Now, I can allow myself to simply feel it—not try to change it. The depth and range of all those experiences have shaped and molded me, hopefully, into a woman who cares and has compassion. I have seen and felt what I once would have believed were unbearable things; now I stand with others who have experienced the same things. We look into each others eyes and we know each other, know what we are feeling, know what we wake up to each morning and what we feel in the last moments before we drift off to sleep. Though I have lived a life I would never wish for my own child, in this moment it all seems as if it has served an important purpose.

"Stand if you have a college degree, if you own your own company, if you have ever been fired from a job. Stand if you have had a life-threatening illness and recovered. Stand if you have ever lived alone. Stand if you have ever lived in a foreign country. Stand if you have ever failed in your business..." And on and on.

I see my frailties exposed in this simple ritual of standing up. I see my capacity born of the life I have lived. I can be of service to another because I've been there. I know you intimately because I know myself; and I love who you are because I know where you stand.

SAYING YES TO CHANGE THROUGH RITUAL

If recognition is the process by which the tribe mirrors an individual back to himself, then ritual is the process of reflecting life's stages back to the individual and to the tribe. All of life's big passages involve a form of death, leading, we hope, to transformation. In many cultures that transition is honored, just as gardeners honor the fact that a field must lie fallow between plantings. In the space between passages we may need to mourn, to share that grieving process with others, and to celebrate what we are moving toward. Most of us have been conditioned to deny the death, to get right back to work, to put it all behind us and get on with the business of life.

The Taoists of ancient China taught that change is the only constant in life. They taught how to be gracefully open and present with change. Completion and wholeness were in every moment, and a person could be at peace only by learning to focus on the present, rather than the past or the future. But how have we in the West been educated for dealing with change? How do we educate our children about it? It seems that we struggle with change, have little patience with it, and in fact do everything we can to keep life predictable, constant, and under our control.

We grow up with false expectations, or no expectations at all, of how the heart, the body, and the mind—the whole person—is going to face what life's changes demand of us. We may feel inadequate when a task with which we're confronted doesn't go as smoothly as it seemed to in the textbook we read in school. That misunderstanding indicates our lack of real preparedness for living, something missing in our set of basic life skills. When confronted with change, many of us dig in our heels, or try to pull the covers over our heads. We tend to value comfort and safety, thus making choices that may not best develop us to grow into something new.

Most rituals take us through a symbolic enactment of the change we face. In doing so, we and our communities align with the transformational process.

LIFE'S PASSAGES

In tribal life we celebrate passages with symbolic rituals. We know that at certain ages our lives change. For instance, as we move from childhood to adolescence, we can no longer expect our parents to soothe our wounds. As we move from adolescence to young adulthood, we are expected to solve our own problems, gather our skills, take a husband or wife, and responsibly create our own lives. In tribe there are rituals and ceremonies that mark our passage from one stage to another, while also announcing to the entire village that we are embracing the next phase. Taking our cues from the ritual, we change, and so does the way that the village relates to us. Having been initiated through the ritual, different behaviors are expected from us. Members of the tribe begin teaching us new things, relating to us differently in this new stage of life.

I DESIGNED A coming-of-age ritual for my godson. It was a ritual in which forces far beyond our comprehension were called upon to support his transition from boyhood to manhood. My godson, who was fifteen years old at the time, lived with his mother and two older sisters in a small town in the Berkshires. Because his father lived thousands of miles away, he had no immediate male role model.

His mother agonized about this. She tried to be everything her son needed, but she realized that assisting his transition into manhood was beyond her capacity. Indeed, she had begun to realize that this passage required her to let go of him.

At this point she asked if I would design a coming-of-age ritual for him. She knew that in designing it I could draw on the wealth of wisdom held by the many men I had met in my personal development work.

While I was designing the ritual, the only thing I told my godson was that he needed to set aside the appointed date and time. He was told nothing else, other than that he should begin thinking about any questions or issues he might like to direct to the guidance, wisdom, or support of older men.

Looking back, I appreciate how those several weeks in advance of the ritual were crucial, and how important it was for us to tell him nothing. That not knowing, that sitting in the tension, helped to get things stirring within his psyche. Outwardly, of course, he was blowing it off. His friends kidded him about it. But inwardly the ritual had already begun.

On the afternoon of the appointed day, I showed my god-son the place in the forest where he was to go that evening. One half-hour before the appointed time, I met with two men who my godson knew and respected. We built a roaring fire in the pitch-black night at the ritual site, and started drumming. We waited for my godson.

At first, his mother had planned to accompany him, but at the last minute she realized this wasn't something she could help him do. She later described how difficult it was for her to watch her son walk into the forest alone, into the dark night. The ritual was having an impact on her, too.

When my godson arrived at the ritual site, we invited him to sit at the fire and begin drumming with us. I suggested that this was the time for us to invite into the space any of our male for-bears. We entered into a long, trance-like silence, interrupted only by our spoken invitations.

After nearly an hour, we moved to the next phase of the ritual. The three of us moved about 30 feet back from the fire and out of earshot of the other. My godson was invited to come sit with each one of us in turn. During this time he could ask any question, seek any guidance or wisdom, in complete confidential-ity. He spent about 10 or 15 minutes speaking with each one of us. We then returned to sit by the fire. As this phase of the ritual ended, we were all gathered once again around the fire.

In the last phase, we asked my godson to lie down on the ground by the fire, and the three of us lifted him up. As we rocked him back and forth in the night, we asked him to feel what it was like to be supported by older men. We ended after a few minutes in a group embrace.

We walked back to his house in silence, and nothing more was said that evening. Indeed, little has been said about it since. But I know it had an impact. One of the most powerful testaments to this was the attitude of my godson's friends in the days after-wards. Instead of making fun of him and the ritual, as they had in advance of it, some of them admitted they were envious, and wished the men in their lives would have done the same for them!

The three of us older men were impacted, as well. Part of being a man is being a mentor to younger men, and my godson had gifted me with that opportunity.

Where are the modern day rituals that take us past such thresholds? We all feel the effect of the loss of such rites of passage.

Such rituals help us accept new forms and structures into our lives. We're reminded we are not alone, as we have seen others before us make the very change we face. We've seen their struggles and their victories, have seen them grieve what they are leaving and move on successfully. Having seen it happen to those who went before us, we would know that this change leads not just to death, but to the birth of a larger potential. With this understanding we can welcome the transition. We don't whine or complain as the whole tribe, our parents included, relates to us differently. In fact, they actually nurture us and demand that we change, having been there themselves. We now take on different parts in the village life, with new status, new responsibilities, new obligations, and new rewards.

For example, we often resist growing older. In Western culture, age is seen as a weakness, a failing, a loss of capacity to be resisted and feared. Imagine if we lived in a society where the mature executive actually understood that, as he aged, his whole being was pulling him away from the pressures of power, and to the exploration of the feminine values of life. As his body began to grow softer, more feminine, breasts and waist becoming larger, he would know that he was moving toward the completion stage of his life. He would appreciate that the inclusion of his emotions and feelings would bring the fulfillment of his soul. If he hadn't seen his elders make this passage before him, if this passage hadn't been named, then his loss of power might be devastating to him, his aging simply marking his final end. Instead, this transition would be a welcome opening, a joyous movement into the next rich stage of his life.

PARTNERING WITH OUR INITIATIONS

We don't have to go out into life looking for initiation; rather, life itself initiates us. It rips us out of one stage and into another. It tears away the veils of innocence and reminds us that life is awesome and powerful. Like the chicken that must peck its way out of the shell to develop the neck muscles it needs to feed itself, life demands that we partner with our initiations if we are to have the capacities that we need to grow.

I'm reminded of an experience I (Jodi) had last summer while sitting with a group of Westerners on the banks of a sacred river in Katmandu. As we arrived at the river, preparations were being made for a cremation. Nearby (within 10 feet), children were playing and women were carrying water and food on their heads, on their way to prepare the evening meal. Meanwhile, the family of the deceased gathered at the shore of the river. The widow was in the shadows, attended by the women, as the men first bathed in the river and then prepared the wood. The widow was a young woman, her husband most likely dying at a young age. The men came for her, and in her grief she was walked over to the cremation site to spread red powder on the area where the fire would be lit. As she spread the powder, she broke down over the horror of her loss.

The group of people I was with wanted to leave immediately—they told me that they didn't want to watch something so unpleasant. I couldn't budge from my seat, but instead looked on, privileged to be witnessing this ritual, so moved to be looking directly into the face of grief and loss. I wanted to know it. I felt my heart swelling as I watched this woman's agony, painfully aware of the losses in my own life that had never been ritualized so richly and completely. I could feel what it would mean to me to be part of the tribe that day. They would see this woman over the next months and years, see how her life would change and develop. They would watch her children grow without their father. They would witness her rebuilding her life. As I watched, I could feel how unprepared I was to deal with loss and death. I saw how important it was for this woman to not only ritualize her husband's death, but to acknowledge through her participation in his cremation that she was being initiated. The other Westerners I was with were gone at the first hint of discomfort. I was transfixed. I had to know.

Initiations can be dangerous passages. They are the rending and tearing of a veil that separates one state of consciousness from another. They are life-changing. If we valued initiation we would open our arms in prayer that the tribe would teach us how to surrender, how to stand firm in the unknown, how to risk, how to be unattached and deeply care at the same time. A tribe would bring its wisdom to these teachings; the tribe would hold us while we surrendered to the teachings of life.

Without a tribe there is no safe place for our initiations, no one who has come before us, no path to point to, no reason even for the suffering and the shedding of old forms. Persistence, balance, self-trust, discipline, capacity, the ability to find resource, the ability to ask for help and to offer it—all of these emanate from our initiations.

In so many of our travels we have seen beautiful tribal rituals that prepare individuals for change. There is a Hindu ritual from Bengal that Joseph Campbell describes in *A Joseph Campbell Companion*:

"The ritual is to prepare a woman to let go of her strongest connection... that of herself with her son. Over a series of years, the family chaplain, the guru, comes and asks her for some valuable thing that she must give him. It starts with some of her jewelry... about the only possessions she has... and then she has to give up certain food that she likes. She has to learn to be quit of that which she values. Then comes the time when her son is no longer a little boy, and by then, she has learned how to say that the most precious thing in her life can go."[1]

Without this type of education, it is almost impossible for us to be responsive to life's passages—what each passage requires us to release, receive, and embrace. Whether it's a mother who must learn how to let go of her teenage son, a newly promoted vice-president in business who must learn new responsibilities, or a young married couple who are learning how to navigate their lives together, life asks us to mature in order to successfully negotiate changes. At these critical times in our lives, there is often a strong pull to return to an earlier way of being, one that we know we can handle, where the rules are clear and where we can predict what is going to happen. Yet, initiation requires us to let go and open to the mystery of change.

We can't expect to live a mature emotional existence without the rites of passage that signal we are no longer children, and have moved into manhood or womanhood. We need the rituals that alert a family and entire community to relate differently to the person who has moved from one stage to another. How many young adults go off to college, gain a sense of themselves, and are then greeted by parents who continue to relate to them as if they were still the child who left home four years before? And who helps the parent through the transition—to let go of the child, to relate newly to them, and to be with the grief of the loss for themselves? We don't know how to be with life because we aren't taught. In most families, such things are rarely even mentioned.

It's not that we wouldn't be willing to discuss life's passages, or even perform necessary rituals to acknowledge them. The problem is that in many cases we are unable to articulate the need, and even if we could, we wouldn't know what to do about it. So we grieve alone in the privacy of our homes, or friends offer advice to make us feel better. But mainly, we handle the changes by moving as quickly as we can back into the old routine, where we find a sense of security. We get right back into the saddle at work. Or we drop back into our old habits of relating to people.

We have developed coping mechanisms, but we are not really wiser for the living of our lives. The rituals of a tribe and a culture orient the individual to the sacred nature of life. Devoid of these rites and rituals, we fear life, and resist or ignore change, rather than embrace it.

RITUAL ISN'T ONLY RELIGIOUS

Through ritual we are able to pay homage to our tribe, and honor being part of life. Ritual is any step that moves us from our individual experience toward an awareness of how our own life is interwoven with other lives, and with life itself. Ritual coalesces community, cuts across all lines, boundaries, and partitions to bring us to the core of ourselves as part of the mystery. We've all experienced ritual. We go to a ballgame, and the entire crowd stands as one body and sings the national anthem, and we are moved. Even if we have no particular feeling for the ritual as a patriotic gesture, we are moved as these many individuals form a single voice, if only for a moment. Or we walk by a church where a bride and groom are taking their wedding vows, and we can't help but be linked to something beyond ourselves. Ritual brings us together. It is an expression that says, "I am part of this intention." Participating in ritual asks us to step into our lives consciously.

I recall the first time I (Carole) witnessed a birth. A friend of mine was about to have her second baby. She was a midwife by profession, so for her the event was a rather everyday experience. She had invited eight people, none of whom knew each other. One evening I got the call to come to the hospital: my friend was in labor. When I arrived, I stepped into her room and the atmosphere was like a cocktail party. There were several journalists who had never met, each working for a different publication. They vied for who was most impressive, who was most important, each trying to outdo the other. Then my friend went into labor in earnest! This child came fast and furious. In what seemed like a moment, all the inflated egos gave way to a gathering in awe. Where there had been boasting and storytelling, there was now only the hush of one breath, the beating of one heart, as the group came together at the foot of her bed to receive this miracle into the world. The moment of this baby's birth brought us together in grace. It became a communion of the highest in each of us. Ritual can do the same.

I (Carole) grew up divided between my upper middle-class Jewish family, going to temple on the Sabbath, and my second family, our maid Alice, who had taken me in like a stray animal in the wake of my mother's illness. When I was living in the ghetto with Alice we attended her Baptist church. I recall the excitement of getting ready for services each Sunday. Instead of the usual drug dealing and arguments going on in the streets, everyone spent their time washing, putting on their finest clothes, making sure there was food for the after-church meal. I would watch Alice and her sister Rhea get ready, carefully bobby-pinning their hair into frayed straw hats, ironing the same stained and worn dresses they had been wearing to church for years. They had so little, but when it came time to get ready for church, to enter the Sunday ritual, every moment was pure devotion. People poured out from everywhere to gather in the church, in their best clothes and manners, for everyone knew that Sunday mornings were sacred. We came together in worship, no judgment, just joining. It was a time of peace, a time to recognize and honor the common bonds of the tribe.

FIRST MOON

A couple of summers ago, I (Jodi) was in Cape Cod with my sister and her family, and Carole and her family. My niece, Liza, had begun menstruating just the month before. My sister had done her best to make sure that Liza knew what she needed to do to take care of herself. One morning we were going to the beach, and Liza started bleeding. I could feel her upset, fear, and discomfort at the new challenges this cycle brought. I looked at her that morning and realized that she was becoming more and more concerned with how she looked. I helped her get ready for the beach, and asked her a lot of questions about how she was doing with what was happening. It became clear that the situation was distressing her. She had no context for the miracle of what her body was announcing it was now able to do. Her life hadn't changed on the outside, which made it doubly difficult to have any acknowledgment of her transformation into a young woman. As my sister struggled with how difficult it was to be the mother of a teenager, wondering what had happened to her sweet little girl, she was hardly the one who would be celebrating Liza's change. She was struggling with her own initiation, having her tears witnessed by women who had survived raising teenagers!

94

Later that day, Carole began looking for a gift for Liza. She bought her a beautiful necklace, the kind a young woman would wear, not one that was suited for a child. She took Liza for a walk, gave her the gift, and talked with her. Liza came back from that walk beaming, proudly displaying the necklace for all to see. This simple ritual honored the change in her body that had already taken place, and seeded the possibility that she could begin to participate more fully with her maturation.

A WOMAN'S RITUAL FOR HER FATHER

I AWOKE FROM A dream in the late afternoon. In the dream, I was a little girl dancing with her father as the sun was setting. I felt loved. I can't remember feeling that way since I was five years old and my father left my mother.

My father had died six months earlier. We never had a chance to get to know each other, yet now I missed him terribly.

Later that evening, while the group gathered in session, I found the courage to hike up the mountain alone. I knew it was time to lay my father to rest. I created an altar to my father on the ground around me, inside a circle I made of rocks. Within the circle I laid out some clay objects I had made which symbolized our relationship.

I sat on the side of the mountain for hours, as if I was with my Dad, recalling many events from my childhood. I could feel how much he loved me. I remembered toys he had made for me, being carried on his shoulders, and his laughter. All those memories came flooding back, memories that had been closed to me for years. I felt overwhelmed by his love for me and grief that I was not able to feel that love while growing up.

I spoke to my Dad that night on the mountain. I told him how much I missed him in my life. I told him about my dreams and shared my experiences of growing up. I told him know how much pain I felt because we hadn't had a relationship. I knew my Dad was there on the mountain listening to me. I felt his sorrow too. I cried his and my tears into the earth. As the sun finally set, we danced. We whirled around, and I knew that I would be okay. I could go on with my life knowing my father had loved me as much as I loved him.

I walked down in the dark feeling alive. I had left my father on the mountain, but found him in my life. I was received into the loving arms of my tribe, waiting at the bottom of the hill for me. To complete the ritual, I danced open-armed with them, feeling myself anew.

A MODERN DAY TRIBAL WEDDING

Recently I (Carole) officiated at my friends Bob and Hilary's wedding. In the beginning of the ceremony, Bob and Hilary deliberately chose to enact their separation from their parents. The wedding was conducted in a circle, with the bride and groom each accompanied by their mother and father.

The husband and wife-to-be walked to the edge of the circle with their families. There, they turned toward their parents and said, "Thank you for holding me and growing me and supporting me so well. Today I leave the circle of your arms to create that circle for myself with my mate. I hold you inside my heart, always, and today I am no longer your son (or daughter)..."

The parents replied, "I have loved you and will love you forever. I respect you and honor the man (woman) you are. Today I release you as my son (or daughter)."

Having released their parents, the bride and groom gave a gift to each other as a symbol of what they were bringing of themselves to the union. As they offered the gifts this is what they said:

Hilary: "Bob, I'm giving you my body. (She handed him a clay sculpture). I made this body from clay and fired it in a wood kiln. It's broken, it's sexy, it's raw, and it is imperfect. It's my hope and intention that we draw on its wisdom and knowledge in our marriage and that we use its resource over and over again."

Bob: "Hilary, in making a gift for you, I wanted to bring something I felt capable of, also something that I felt awkward at and unsure of myself about. So, I have written a poem. The poem is about how it feels to love you. I feel a little shaky with commitment, so I thought it would be appropriate to have the words etched in stone." (Bob took out a stone tablet.)

Loving you is like a great big sigh...
A settling in, a relaxing into my body.
Walking toward you is like walking home...
A warm home where I can rest and be at ease.

Sitting with you is like sitting by a fire...
Almost hypnotized by your dancing glow.
Being held in your arms is like falling,
Rocking, tenderly drifting deep into my own soul.

Sometimes, when I am very still, I can hear
Your name being whispered softly by my heartbeat.
And I remember that I really have found you—
The one whose name my heart has called all my life.

With my undying love and devotion, Bob.

Those gathered to witness Bob and Hilary's wedding vows that day remembered their own sacred vows, honoring themselves and the partners they had struggled with and loved. Bob and Hilary had a very powerful beginning of their life together, signified and recognized by a ritual that honored what they are and might be together. The ritual set in motion their hopes and dreams for a new life.

TIMELESS GUARDIANS

It is through rites and rituals that we deepen our understanding and our capacity for self-trust, holding steady in the face of the unknown. As we are recognized by others, and in turn recognize them, we feel connected to our tribe and to all who have gone before us. Rituals are the timeless guardians that support us as we let go of one stage of life, and move into the next.

Our initiations and life passages are often difficult, but they lead us to new potential, new birth, and new possibilities; through them we learn to take on life's challenges with grace. Through the initiatory process, accompanied by recognition, rites, and rituals, we move ever closer to the mastery of the art of living.

Voices Of The Tribe

A voice on the initiation of new parenthood:

Dear Friends,

As many of you know, Zachary Allen Kammen-Harwood was born on February 26th. His arrival in our lives has certainly been an incredible initiation. I marvel at the mystery that he is… so close to God, it seems. And am often shocked by what the reality is demanding of me! Becoming a parent is a significant shift in consciousness.

Watching his first few weeks is a lesson again for me: that life presents many trials and initiations, full of pain and learnings to be encountered. For Zach, just growing a digestive system is such difficult work. He finally learns to turn his head, and more of the world opens up!

And the initiations for Bob and I are just as exacting. Marriage ceases to be just about the two of us and has become about the gifting of our vital life energy to the baby. Work stops in an instant when Zach cries, dinners eaten hurriedly—if at all. As I write this, I am typing with one hand and rocking his cradle with my other. And, oh, the sleepless nights that feel like they will stretch on forever, as all of you seasoned parents must remember! But little by little, we begin to discern a hunger cry from a cranky cry, and therein is the true initiation. In the midst of all the chaos the Mother inside of me is emerging like a new, young spring shoot. I get a glimpse of what is emerging in me from this process—Mother, who can care not only for my son, but for my own needy children within as well. Perhaps this is the great Plan of Life, that we heal ourselves as we gift a new being into existence.

This transition into new parenthood seems truly to be about the archetypal shift for me into mother, protector, caregiver. It is not always a welcome or easy shift. I am learning that real life—its joys and sufferings and compromises—is my true teacher—and that this is my daily meditation for this moment.

This initiation brings with it a trusting of my body's wisdom. Pregnancy was incredible—watching my belly and breasts grow large, carrying a child, and preparing to sustain and nourish him, once in the world. As I trust my body, I find my Woman's wisdom which has been locked up forever, waiting for the time to release her gifts. As she does, Zach and I learn how to be with each other.

I have received so much support from all of you... love, prayers, gifts to welcome Zach into the world. I am moved by all of you who came forward to embrace us in the arms of this community. I thank the many women who made this passage before me, and offered and continue to offer wisdom, and a strong sense of support seasoned with the deepest knowing.

—Carole Kammen

This is a voice from a woman's 50th birthday ritual:

HONORING MY LIFE

I feel birthdays are a time to recognize and honor life. My 50th birthday was spent away from home. It started with a wonderful day with my husband. When we got back to our room, I felt that there was something more that needed to be done. It was late after we finished packing for our long flight the next day, but I felt the need to really go deeply into the significance of my birthday. Just what did it mean? What did I appreciate after 50 years of living? And then I began to journal:

"I'm thankful for all the experiences I've had. I appreciate my spirit of adventure that keeps me trying new things and taking risks. I appreciate my strong body that has walked many miles, overcome illness, is sensual, enjoys food, soft breezes and the smell of Star Jasmine in the air."

As I wrote this letter to myself, the tears welled in my eyes; the deep emotion anchoring the feelings of appreciation. The feeling was not of sorrow. Tears appear from a myriad of impulses not related to reason as we usually think of it. When I first started to cry, my husband comforted me. I explained that I wasn't sad, I was feeling my life in gratefulness, the emotion signifying that the message was getting through to all parts of self, I REALLY AM GRATEFUL.

—Rachel Carpenter

6

THE FOURTH VALUE: EDUCATION

Give your ears, hear the sayings. Give your heart to understand them...

—*Amenemope, c. 11th century B.C.*

Storytelling, you know, has a real function. The process of the storytelling is itself a healing process, partly because you have someone there who is taking the time to tell you a story that has great meaning to them. They're taking the time to do this because your life could use some help, but they don't want to come over and just give advice. They want to give it to you in a form that becomes inseparable from your whole self. That's what stories do. Stories differ from advice in that, once you get them, they become a fabric of your whole soul. That is why they heal you.

—*Alice Walker*[1]

A YOUNG INITIATE is studying to become a monk. He decides to go to a remote island for the solitude he believes he needs in order to concentrate on learning his incantations and mantras, which he will have to know for his final initiation. He rows off to the island, and spends many days repeating the mantras over and over again. One day he decides to take a break. He goes for a short walk to the other side of the island, and all the while he is walking, he is chanting and reciting the phrases that he must know. He happens upon a poor fisherman, who waves and says, "Hello there, what is that you are chanting over and over again?"

Irritated, the young monk dismisses him, saying, "Nothing that you would know. I am studying for an important exam, and if I pass it I will be a spiritual leader."

The old man inquires if there is anything he can do to help the young monk, but the boy just laughs him away. During the rest of the young monk's stay, he decides that he would indeed be able to learn his lessons much more readily if he were to teach them to the old fisherman. He would truly prove his worthiness if he could teach a person as ignorant as this! So he engages the old man, and each day gives him a lesson, admonishing him over and over again that he must get the phrases exactly right. Finally, it is time for the initiate to leave. He bids the old fisherman farewell, the man thanks him for the lessons, then helps the boy push off from the island in his little boat.

The initiate has rowed about a half mile from shore when he hears the voice of the old man calling to him. He turns around, and to his amazement, the old man is running *right on top of the water!* He is calling out to him, "Young man, young man! Please wait. Tell me one more time how I should pronounce that last phrase you taught me."

Like the monk discovered with the fisherman, many of our most important teachers aren't found in classrooms. Nor do they give lectures or write books. They're often right beside us, at the supermarket checkout counter, in the seat next to us on the plane, on subways, or living across the hallway in our apartment building. They might be the techies just down the hall from the manager's office, or they might be waiting in the lunch lines of the office cafeteria. We miss so much of the education that would truly nurture us, because in our culture we have not placed a high value on an education in the personal and spiritual realms.

We need to be open to receiving the wisdom that others around us offer, as we need to accept the responsibility of educating others. We live so close to our truth that we cannot always see its value to others, and in this respect we are all blind to our own gifts of knowledge. The Sufis say that there are three lines of self-development:

1. Know yourself.
2. Know the other as he is to himself.
3. Transmit the information.

As we teach what we know, it truly becomes a part of us.

KNOWLEDGE SHARED

In modern society, education in the spiritual and emotional realms is hidden. Parents raise the children in the privacy of the nuclear family. But the experience of two individuals, no matter how capable, is just not enough for a child to become completely educated. To grow into our fullest potential, we need the wisdom of many different persons. We need to be in their presence, so they can model for us the widest range of possibilities.

Once we're participating in a tribal process, the competitive heat that drives many of our endeavors lessens. Instead of seeing knowledge as a way of getting the upper hand, we begin to experience a shift of consciousness, seeing that what is achieved is meant to be shared. It becomes possible to see achievement not as a threat, but as an asset. Whereas we were once proud of what we knew but ashamed of our ignorance, our ignorance now becomes a door that swings open to welcome in others' wisdom.

Each person's full participation is part of an expanding whole. When we understand that our sacred responsibility is to educate the tribe, we begin to freely offer what we know. We name what we've experienced, and we're generous with information about our own mistakes, struggles, and failures.

In modern life, we extol individualism above the tribe; we are responsible to no one but ourselves. Though we gain a measure of personal freedom, we're also shackled by this ethic which drums into our heads and hearts that our greatest strength will be found in serving ourselves first.

To see how this works, let's contrast life in our Hmong village with life in New York City. I (Jodi) remember living in a large apartment building on the upper east side of Manhattan. I rarely talked with or even saw my neighbors, though we lived side by side, separated only by thin walls. There were probably four hundred people living in that building. I didn't know a single one of them! Nor could I connect a single name with a face.

Many nights I'd sit in my living room and think how in that building, at any given time, there had to be at least twenty families finally removing the protective child-proof door locks from kitchen and bathroom cabinets, while at the same time there were a dozen families trying to figure out how to child-proof their apartments to make them safe for their toddlers. Not only that, many families would be bringing their children's outgrown clothes or toys downstairs to the trash, just as five other families were on their way out to the toy store to purchase similar toys for their younger kids. And thirty single people would be sitting alone at home every Friday night, wondering how to meet new friends. At least five people would be struggling with the recent death of a loved one, while at least a dozen people had actually been through that experience in the last two years. There would undoubtedly be twenty women trying to understand what their bodies were doing as they approached the early days of menopause, while thirty women in the building were through that stage of life, and at least half of them would willingly share their stories with the others. We only talked to the doorman when we entered the building, never turning to see if perhaps, living right next door to us, was the person we most needed to learn from or teach.

Tribal education gets lost as we widen the distance between ourselves and our neighbors. In the small Hmong village where we sat that day many years ago, we saw a form of education that embodies all of life, where every participant is both student and teacher. In both roles they communicate who they are, what is expected, and how they experience their lives. Through this exchange, both persons not only learn the skills required to participate in their community, but they can share the feelings which come from their use of those skills in daily life.

So often we want to share with others but we hold back, because just under the surface are the implications or outright assertions that we shouldn't burden others with our issues, or others can't be trusted anyway, or that sharing our experiences with others takes something away from us, or revealing something about ourselves is nobody's business but our own.

In every community, company, and family there is a wealth of knowledge, but we've relegated education to the "experts." We focus mostly on acquiring skills and ideas, separated from the understanding born of experience. In the process we have forgotten that knowledge in the personal, emotional, and spiritual realms is an evolutionary requirement. We can't get this education in the classroom.

How sad it is that today we neglect a source of strength that for tens of thousands of years has allowed learning to take place. It's as though, in the process of designing the architecture of our modern culture, we've misplaced the key that can unlock our human potential: that only when we place our skills and our knowledge within the greater context of life events can we be complete.

The father who's at work thirty miles from home, triumphant in his latest success, is separated from his young son, who will never see the emotion expressed in his father's face, never share the tense moments of his father's uncertainty which are integral to the process of this man's life. The son will never see his father dig deep within himself and summon the courage to persist in his endeavor. So this son never has the emotional learning intrinsic to his father's life; he'll never have that wisdom to draw upon when, as an adult, this son is called into the same experiences.

Similarly, a young woman will lie writhing on her living room floor, in grief following the signing of her divorce papers, even as twenty other women do the same within a few miles of her. No one who has already negotiated this difficult passage will hold these grieving women, will speak to them of the pain that feels as if it will last an eternity, but then like the end of a long winter, will burst forth in new life. In tribe, these women would have lived in accord with the natural flow of life. They would know that the natural flow is passage and change. If they lived in accord with life, life would teach them that. They would see it, feel it. They wouldn't even need to be told. The tribe would hold them while life educated and initiated them to move forward, beyond their grief, into the next stage of life.

Each passage we complete not only teaches us, it also turns us into teachers and mentors, signaling us to share the path. The act of mentoring allows us to really explore and honor what we know, to embrace and validate all our life experiences, regardless of what they are. As we mentor others, we learn that life is not truly complete until all that we have learned has been given away.

Thinking tribally requires an enormous shift of consciousness for those of us living in today's world. In our "me-and-mine" society we see other's successes as our failures. We perceive life from a place of scarcity, where if anybody gets what they are seeking they're taking away from us. Like the sperm competing with other sperm to fertilize the egg, we act as if there's only one prize, that only one can enter through the door of success. In tribal consciousness we're all informed, inspired, heightened, and strengthened by the growth and success of any tribe member.

MONKEY SEE, MONKEY DO

When I (Carole) was pregnant with my son, Zachary, I was both overjoyed and terrified. I had not grown up around children, and unless something changed quickly in my life, Zachary would be the first baby I had ever held! Friends said I should prepare myself to nurse Zachary by hiring a breast-feeding consultant. So I did, although I truly wondered why such a role was needed. Wouldn't my body just instinctively know how to do this?

When the consultant came to my home, she addressed this issue of maternal instincts first. She told me, "You might think that your body should just know what to do to feed a child, and it does. But in today's world, women are often out of touch with their bodies. Even if you were in touch, you have not, I presume, sat among breast-feeding women. When the time comes to feed Zachary, will you know the position to hold him in? Will you be prepared to carry out what your body tells you to do?"

She told me about a young gorilla who, from a very early age, had been raised in a zoo, separated from her tribe. When she came of age she was introduced to a mate, and in time she became pregnant. When the baby finally came, the mother seemed bewildered and frightened. She was tender and caring with the little one but refused to breast feed her infant, so in spite of regular bottle feeding by the zoo staff the little one was withering away.

Zoo psychologists reasoned that, because the young gorilla mother had been raised in isolation, she'd never witnessed breast-feeding. If she could somehow see other mothers nursing, perhaps she'd learn how to do it herself. But where was the zoo going to find a gorilla mother for her model? Then someone had a brilliant idea: they brought in several lactating human mothers and their infants. Sitting near the young gorilla's cage, these mothers held their own infants to their breasts and fed them. Within a short period of time, the gorilla mother, modeling the behavior of these humans, pressed her own infant to her breast, and at last began nursing as nature had intended.

This story, and others like it, are profound reminders that we can learn so much about living as a direct witness, by hearing each other's stories, by being guided by people whose knowledge comes through their own life experience. Often, we simply have to be in the presence of the event for the inherent knowledge and wisdom to come through.

Though modern life has given us much, we're also desperately in need of certain kinds of information we once received from tribal life. In her writings, Hillary Clinton touches on a theme that echoes back through the history of humanity: it takes a village to raise a child. Our own lives have become so severed from this truth we don't even realize many of us are reinventing the wheel at every passage, covering the same ground others before us have covered millions of times. If only we could slow down, watch, and learn.

A CHAPTER FROM THE TRIBAL TEXTBOOK

SIX MONTHS earlier Greg had sat in a room similar to this, with a gathering of people that were also similar. Different stories had been told, and the faces were different, but the hearts were the same now. He had dreamed of the day his twin brother and their father might join him in a sacred circle. First his brother Jeff came to a workshop, and Jeff, in turn, had gotten their dad to come to this one. It had always been like that. Jeff could get Dad to do almost anything, and Greg could always get Jeff moving.

On this day, Jeff and Greg, twins, sat across from their father. All three men shared certain recognizable characteristics. The three men, of course, were familiar with their similarities. But to the witnesses in the circle, the likenesses were uncanny.

The two brothers had always closely identified with each other. But now, as they sat across from their father, near enough to feel each other's breath, they recognized and identified with he who had fathered them, who had always seemed so huge, ten feet tall. For the first time, they noted he was actually just like them, not only looking like them, but their size as well.

"I did the best I could," the father was saying. "I am so sorry for the places I fell short." Tears streamed down his face. "I didn't know it mattered. It seemed to embarrass you when I showed up to throw around a baseball with you and your friends. I thought you wanted to be left alone. I wanted you to have your own life. I didn't know you wanted my help. I wish I had shown more patience. I'm sorry for letting you down." Suddenly, he was sobbing, "I did the best I could!"

Greg felt himself moving between two powerful urges. The most unbelievable to him was the urge to curl up in his father's lap. At the same time, he yearned to rush up and hold his father in his arms, to comfort him, to let him know it was okay. He could hardly believe the words that were coming out of his father's mouth, words he had wanted to hear his entire life: his father telling of his love, his father sharing his pride.

Greg heard himself speaking and wasn't sure where his words were coming from. It was as if his heart were speaking. He'd always wanted to talk to his father like this, but men in their family just didn't do that. "I never really knew who you were," he said. "I always wanted to know. I still want to know. I wanted other kids I knew to see me with you. I was so proud you were my dad. I still am."

Greg and his brother knew that each moment of this experience was changing them, that they would never be the same again. Their father had become a man to them today, and they had become men to themselves. Nobody in that room had ever read a book or gone to a class that could have taught them what they learned that day, from a man in the presence of the tribe asking for forgiveness from his sons, and admitting where his failings had been. Greg's father couldn't go back and redo those years, of course. But every man and woman who sat in the room that day, every person with children, had the possibility of going home and doing it differently, changing what is. Many of the people said they were relieved to see they weren't the only ones who had fallen short with their children, and perhaps they could now live with themselves more easily having witnessed this.

Tribe is the container for family, and tribal education honors the process of trial and error. Failures are inevitable, and they actually serve the education of all those around us. Parents working alone can't possibly be all the archetypes—the models we need for growth.

They can't possibly pass along the rich, expansive wisdom of the ages contained in tribal consciousness. Spacious and far-reaching, the tribe relieves the burden placed on the family to be everything.

MENTORSHIP—LEADING AND BEING LED

There is a short documentary film we love about two men running a race, on a very beautiful yet challenging ten-mile trail in northern California. Called the Dipsea Trail, it goes from the floor of a redwood forest, up the side of Mt. Tamalpais, then down to the ocean, over rugged twisting terrain.

One of the two men in the film is blind; the other is his sighted guide. The film opens with the men getting ready to run in the midst of several hundred runners. We hear the sharp report of the starting gun, and then see a close-up of the blind man running behind the sighted man, his hands lightly touching his guide's hips. They ascend a steep trail, navigating the treacherous protruding roots that present hazards to even the sighted runners. People pass the two men as the race progresses.

The sighted man is caring, aware of his partner. The two are constantly communicating—cursing as they slip or trip, laughing as they get underway again. The guide offers encouragement, the blind runner tells jokes, friendly jibes are traded, and steady feedback exchanged. As the terrain changes, the sighted man calls out what's ahead; the blind man acknowledges, sometimes urging his guide to go faster, sometimes slower. At one point, the blind man stumbles and the sighted man waits for him to get up, asks him if he's okay, then shouts, "Come on, let's go!"

The guide stays aware of his partner's abilities and limitations; there is no sense of coddling him. The blind man follows instructions, asks for clarification, and stays focused on their shared goal: to finish the race. At one point, the two men turn on to a divergent path, and the sighted man says, "We've just taken an easier path." The blind man says, "That's good," and the sighted man replies, "It's much longer." He's aware of the effort and energy this challenge requires from them. The film ends with a freeze frame of the two men crossing the finish line—triumph across their faces.

As people watch this film, they are moved by what the intention and goals of the mentor, the sighted man, must be. For him it's obviously not about running the race, although he is a seasoned runner; he's run this race for himself countless times. As a mentor, he is making something possible for the blind man that the blind man could not experience without him. Yet clearly he also needs the blind man, to share his skills and to have the opportunity to experience the difference he can make.

Those who view the film are equally as impressed with how the blind man participates with his mentor. He is available, open, willing, and trusting of what is being offered to him. He too brings his best—he clearly isn't being dragged down the trail! The viewers witness a bond formed during the run that goes way beyond that of one man helping a less fortunate one; they see a powerful equality, a joining of courage and cooperation. After watching this film, people are often filled with a different perspective on the meaning of mentorship.

THE GOLDEN EGG

Each passage we make, each goal we reach, each piece of life we have struggled with, gives us material that enriches us as teachers or mentors. The act of mentoring allows us to explore, appreciate, and honor what we know. In tribal consciousness, we are each informed, inspired, and strengthened by any tribe member who shares their experiences.

When I (Jodi) go to a company and teach them a model for mentorship, both morale and productivity increase. They experience how each person's success strengthens the entire team.

During the planning phases of our first corporate mentorship program, I wrestled with an interesting question: Why would someone want to mentor? If they are in a powerful position, they already know they are needed and they have job security. What would motivate them to be a mentor? Furthermore, mentoring can be challenging, requiring a skill they might not have, and taking on an extra responsibility would probably make their lives harder for a while, not easier.

Then I realized why I was uncertain: I was approaching the question from a me-and-mine consciousness. From this limited point of view, of course your gain is my loss, my knowledge my safety, and of course I'm afraid that if I mentor you, you will become more skilled than I am and outdo me!

One of my associates reminded me of the story about the goose who laid the golden eggs. Surely, our first responsibility is to preserve the health of the goose so that she can supply us forever with her golden eggs. But my associate added a new twist to the story. She asked, "Who is more valuable, the goose that can lay golden eggs, or the goose that can teach other geese to lay their own golden eggs?" Her question brought me back to an important lesson: in any company, family, or community, a mentor can often be much more valuable than a single contributor.

OFFERING OURSELVES AS MENTORS

KAREN KNEW that she wanted to see Dan on her way to the airport for her first business trip. Two months ago she didn't have this much responsibility, and she wasn't sure she had the confidence to troubleshoot problems, create solutions, and mobilize people into action. Until recently, her career had been going nowhere.

Dan had mentored Karen for the last two months, and she wanted to let him know how much it had meant to her to have him believe in her more than she did herself. Not that he ever said much to her. But he would have that "you can do it" look in his eyes that she had seen so many times. And he had patiently explained to her terminology and strategy, described the corporate structure, and reviewed her technical plans. The most important teaching for her was watching him in action, staying cool and calm when everyone else around him was getting heated up.

As Dan mentored Karen, he realized that he looked forward to going to work each day. He felt more sure of himself, and he had to admit that he loved getting a chance to offer his skills. He felt clearer today about what he knew and had accomplished professionally than ever before. Lately, people had been stopping by his office, asking for his input on their ideas. Mentorship was bringing out a real love of leadership that he had only dreamed he would one day be able to experience.

This story illustrates the bond experienced in a productive mentorship relationship. Dan cared about Karen's success, communicated clearly, offered encouragement, gave feedback, and described hazards and how to avoid them. Karen, in turn, made herself available to learning from Dan. She was willing to accept the challenges presented to her, follow instructions, ask for clarification when needed, and stay focused on the goal.

Clearly, Dan was motivated by something more than getting Karen up to speed on this new job. In mentoring Karen, Dan used a different skill set than he normally would in his job. Karen offered her mentor the opportunity to share his skills, and experience a new challenge in his life. Both Dan and Karen were enriched by this experience.

BECOMING A LIFE-LONG LEARNER

In tribal life, it's the responsibility of all members to develop themselves as fully as they can, to become capable instruments in service to the tribe. Contrast this to the highly individualized and dismembered way most of us live today, with our emphasis on me-and-mine. In me-and-mine consciousness, I develop myself, by myself, in order to acquire what I want for myself. There's no feedback loop to mirror how my actions affect the larger whole. There's no consideration of how my life might serve others.

Tribal education prepares individuals to live in relationship to a larger reality, one that extends beyond their individual whims. The life skills emphasized in tribe not only maintain the physical balance of the tribe, but the emotional and spiritual balance as well. Education is taken very seriously. The entire clan becomes involved, male and female, young and old. One grows up knowing the value and importance of learning, and as they grow, individuals come to understand that it is their responsibility to impart the teaching, to pass along what they know to others.

We'd like to recommend going beyond just understanding this relationship. Let yourself feel the beauty of it! Put yourself back in the Hmong village and take in the balance of learning and teaching, of wisdom imparted and drawn upon by all, for the benefit of all. Our educational responsibility would not even have to be discussed. It would be so integral to living, so essential, that this way of learning and teaching would be as automatic as breathing—and its value just as evident.

Imagine for a moment that over the next forty-eight hours your task is to learn as much as you can from your life. Then, for the following forty-eight hours, your responsibility would be to offer that knowledge to those around you. To accomplish this you would have to start asking a lot of questions, self-reflecting, staying focused, opening to new ideas, asking for help, emulating those around you, looking for role models, and trying new behaviors. Life would take on a new texture; it would become rich with lessons. You would watch the people around you to see what they offered, with a willingness to move out of your comfort zone, out of the known into the unknown. You'd probably spend a period of time each evening with your family, friends, or spouse reflecting on the learning from the day, wanting to hear about their experiences, and perhaps for a moment see the fullness of a life that has now become your classroom. This is a glimpse into the nature of being a life-long learner, and what it means to have your own education and the education of those around you be part of your sacred participation as a human being.

OUR TEACHERS ARE ALL AROUND US

In the film *Star Wars*, Luke Skywalker wants to become a Jedi, so he is sent to work with the master, Yoda. Many of you will remember that when he reaches the alien world where he will study, the first being he confronts is a small, aging, odd-looking toad. He can't imagine that this could be Yoda; it certainly isn't his image of a person who could teach him to be a great warrior. Yoda has him do all kinds of things he isn't interested in, taking the cocky young Luke through all kinds of trials.

In a culture that has an educational system that teaches us to value what we know and be ashamed of what we don't, we tend to operate in our lives just like the young, uninitiated Luke! Being in a learning process becomes as alien to us as Yoda's world was to Luke when he first arrived. So often, the greatest life teachers are standing right in front of us, while we desperately look around for information.

Wisdom is not imparted to us merely by a high school diploma or a college degree. Life offers us the moments that develop us. In the same way that Luke had to become willing to be taught by Yoda, we must be willing to make the people around us, to make life, our teacher.

TIPS FOR SUCCESS AS A LIFE-LONG LEARNER

1. Have A Beginner's Mind.

The Buddhists have a teaching that's relevant to the practice of being a life-long learner. They talk about approaching life with a beginner's mind. Learning is possible only if we don't think we already know! A beginner's mind leaves us open for fresh discovery. We look for the opportunity to see the familiar in a new light, to learn from the people we hadn't expected to be our teachers, to see new possibilities in something we've done hundreds of times. This practice is most challenging, and most critical, as we move through the events of our lives that seem habitual or predictable.

2. Be Self-Reflective And Self-Monitoring.

A research study done several years ago explored the question, "What makes some people (who begin with equal capacity to learn) more successful learners than others? What are the behaviors they demonstrate that lead to their success?" The study found that successful learners are in a constant process of self-reflection. They spend time each day reviewing their actions, and noticing what they did that lead to successful outcomes. They then take that information and use it well. They repeat the things that work, and they change the behaviors that don't work by trying new things.

3. Take Risks.

The study also found that successful learners are risk takers. Successful learners are willing to take chances. They're willing to try things they haven't before, and most importantly, they're willing to fail, to be wrong, to be clumsy. Failure is inevitable when we are learning. We are so vulnerable during this phase!

4. Learn To Love The Questions.

There is a beautiful writing in Rainer Maria Rilke's *Letters to a Young Poet,* "I beg you to be patient toward all that is unsolved in your heart and try to love the QUESTIONS THEMSELVES like locked rooms and like books written in a very foreign tongue. Do not seek the answers, which cannot be given you because you would not be able to LIVE them. And the point is to live everything... Perhaps you will then gradually, without noticing it, live along some distant day into the answer..."[2]

Gurdjieff taught a wonderful practice that he called "standing before a question." This meant posing a question that has no immediate answer—and standing in the tension of the not knowing. To do this, we have to value the learning process itself, and trust that the questions would lead us to more than we could imagine—instead of our usual demand to have the information we want right now.

Time and again we have found these to be some of the most valuable questions:

What is life teaching me?
How can I participate well?
How can I learn from this?
What am I being given the opportunity to live, learn, develop?
What is this serving?
What is life calling me to?

These are questions whose answers are continually changing. They'd take more than a lifetime to answer fully!

5. Show Up Available To Learn.

We can only begin any of these practices if we are willing to be vulnerable, to value learning first, before the desire to be the absolute best or to accomplish great things. To live in tribe is to see this willingness as our sacred responsibility.

An Open Relationship To Life

Every passing moment offers us something new and unknown. We can choose to approach each one as a threat, to be resisted or conquered, or we can open our hearts and embrace it, reveling with our friends and loved ones in its possibilities, sharing our knowledge and ourselves in a glorious exploration.

Education is not just a school system, and it doesn't stop when our formal training is complete. Whether we're aware of it or not, we're teaching each other and being taught all the time. As we become conscious of this, and open to our responsibility to teach the tribe, we have a reason for learning from our own life events. We consciously choose to act as both teacher and student. We really are different when we're actively trying to teach, or learn. We're alert, more open, more forthcoming, a better listener—and we notice our whole experience of our relationships and our lives begins to change.

Community gatherings for the purpose of recognizing, storytelling, and listening bring tribal education alive again. Over the years, we've loved watching people bring the vibrancy of their lives to the tribes they embrace. Now the clan becomes vital, as the stories and myths to live by come alive.

This is education of the highest order.

Voices Of The Tribe

As I sat in the circle and watched these two men together, I began to wonder, where in a million years would they have ever found their way to each other? Had they passed on the street, they simply would not have even seen each other at all. Yet here they were, two men at opposite ends of the spectrum of a man's life, with so much wisdom and so much healing to offer each other. They, me, and everyone who witnessed that circle of men were forever taught and changed by that experience.

—Tina Benson

Sitting here I realize what being a part of a tribe has given me is the opportunity to experience my impact from others' perspectives, by getting compassionate feedback and learning how to receive it openly. It's often quite painful, but it has brought me more growth than I ever could have had trying to "figure it out" on my own. Having learned from so many different people, my own internal life is richer than it ever was before, and now I treat the world as my teacher.

—Christopher Rosebrook

7

THE FIFTH VALUE: SERVICE

We can do no great things—only small things with
great love.

—*Mother Teresa*

The Sufi opens his hands to the universe
and gives away each instant, free.
Unlike someone who begs on the street for money to survive,
a dervish begs to give you his life.

—*Rumi*

MANY YEARS AGO Jodi and I (Carole) went to India. Traveling halfway around the world, we didn't know what to
expect. But one thing was certain, the experience would
surely have an impact on us. Instantly swept up by the throngs of humanity milling endlessly through the overcrowded streets of Delhi,
we were overwhelmed by a myriad of new sights and sounds. I remember the pungent, exotic smells of spices and curries.

As we walked down one of the alleys outside the market
place, we heard two male voices joined in the most beautiful song.
Guided by the music, we were led through the alley and across a busy
street, where we discovered the source of these wondrous sounds.
There on the side street, facing one another in fetal positions, lay two
leprous men. They were both dressed in what were once white rags,
lying there with gangrenous, rotting limbs, open sores on their arms,
stumps where once had been hands and feet. And they sang! One of

the men led as he sang his chant, and the other answered in harmony. We stood transfixed... immobilized by the horror of their condition and the beauty of their song. They sang and sang. After a while, a well-dressed Indian man approached us, seeing us staring at the singing men. He told us, "They are singing a love song to God, for all to hear. And as the people pass them on the street, they throw a few coins down for them... it is good. They sing to God for all of us, and we give them money so they can keep singing."

Ever since that day, the image of these two lepers singing has stayed in our minds, symbolizing for us the beauty of service and devotion. These men had nothing to give but their love of God and their voices—rich, resonant, and intact. Regardless of the state of their bodies, they still had something to contribute. They were bringing the only gift they had to the Delhi streets, and they gave it with their hearts. Each passerby was touched in some way by the song, the song itself becoming the music for that entire city block.

If we are to create tribe consciously, we will inevitably be led to the question of service. I belong, I am part of this tribe. It contributes to me, recognizes me, educates me, prepares me for life. I then must ask myself, what can I contribute to this tribe that has sustained and nourished me? Inevitably, in cultures that have kept the tribal rites and rituals intact, the young initiate must leave the tribe, go out into the world to test himself, and return again to the village, skilled and ready to contribute. Cut off from the tribe, as we so often are in modern life, we develop only ourselves. We forget to ask, what we are developing ourselves in service to? We don't ask ourselves, "How can I serve the tribe?"

When we feel ourselves to be a meaningful part of tribe, the desire to serve inevitably follows. Actions that contribute come naturally, almost instinctively. Self-love and self-esteem grow easily up from the fertile soil of our positive efforts.

The actions that will best serve the tribe won't always stay the same—they'll change as the needs of the tribe change. We need to stay open to these changes to make sure we're really serving the tribe, and not just ourselves. And knowing who we're really serving can sometimes be tricky. For example, when we have only our own, rigid idea of what serves, or when we want to give so we'll be recognized for our contributions, we're actually serving ourselves first. Even when we deeply believe we're just trying to contribute, we can easily mistake serving ourselves for serving our tribe, simply because we've lived our lives practicing putting our own needs ahead of others'.

So how can we know what or even how to contribute? Here are some questions that, when we reflect upon them, become important guides.

1. What is my tribe consecrated to? What is its sacred purpose?
2. How can I serve that purpose in my own way?
3. What do I have that is needed at this time?

As we mature emotionally and spiritually, our values begin to change. We experience this shift in many different ways. For example, we become less interested in arguing about who's right and who's wrong and ask ourselves instead, "How can I be of service?" What can I do right now to improve the quality of my relationship to this person or this situation? The tribal values of relating become guiding principles, shepherding us in service toward understanding, vulnerability, and good, solid communication.

In tribal life, people living solely for themselves and their own comfort or self-interest don't remain part of the tribe for long. Tribes understand that the health, even the survival of the tribe depends on each member contributing their share. To serve the community is imperative. The goal to serve the community becomes an initiating force that takes us past our insecurities and fears, to what is highest, truest, and best in ourselves.

To truly serve, we must take our direction from something other than our own egos. What exactly does this mean? It might mean letting go of our need to dominate, to exert power over others in an effort to make ourselves more comfortable. It might ask us to see with new eyes some of the things we do to avoid feeling our vulnerability. This would require that we examine the many ways in which we defend ourselves when we feel threatened.

Service isn't the holier-than-thou attitude of the great one bestowing his or her gifts upon the world. Rather, service is devotion. Service is the willingness to love, to be tender and open. Service is the act of opening to our love and our depth of caring, even if we can't tell how that caring will be received or responded to. Ultimately, we find in the depth of our longing to serve there comes the tiniest young bud, a small tender shoot that transforms our caring into action in the world.

Service doesn't emanate from the kind of power most of us are familiar with. Service is powerful, but it doesn't depend on one person exercising their will over another. Moreover, we don't have to create something worthy of the Nobel Peace Prize for service to happen. Acts of service can be simple. They happen when we reach out, when we make an extra effort. They happen in the tiny moments when we see something is needed, and then do something about it.

Service means living with our eyes open, compassionately and accountably. We often shrink when we hear the word "responsibility." It brings up visions of entrapment, imprisonment, or confinement—seemingly the exact opposite of what we are struggling to achieve. But the kind of responsibility we are talking about here is actually the path to freedom of expression, meaning, and purpose.

THE PRESIDENT of the organization was stunned. She sat listening as her staff talked about their renewed commitment, their accountability for their careers, their sense of belonging to something bigger than themselves. They talked about their feeling that no matter how big or small their contribution, what they did was important, and the ways their own work encouraged their peers to bring their best forward.

One woman talked about her efforts to bring a new idea to her manager. The manager at first was uninterested. The woman said, "Six months ago I would have given up. This time, I kept trying. I understood that I was accountable, so I had to keep offering my suggestions when I knew they were important, and I had to learn how to communicate them clearly enough to get them heard."

Another person talked about feeling the impact he had on his entire project team when they had been deadlocked in opposing views the week before. Instead of sitting back and hoping someone else would do something, he gently reminded them that they were all on the same side, working for the same goals. Then he had them each renew their commitment to the project!

One man talked excitedly about how helpful his mentor's coaching had been, and how encouraged he'd felt, particularly when he went back to his peers to talk with them about completing the prototype for a new technology they were developing. The prototype was finally accepted by the company, and installed company-wide! This man was clear that he never could have completed the project without his mentor's commitment, belief, and encouragement.

Every story presented belonged to the whole group.

The president congratulated them all. She told them how much they were modeling the best of the organization's values and vision. She wanted to know exactly what had happened in this "Tribal Practices" program they'd been in. "How can we bottle this so we can share it with others?" This was the tribal dynamic working at its best.

For six months this group had been working together on the tribal practices of Belonging, Recognition, and Education. Through actions such as committing to each others' goals, offering recognition, coaching each other during new experiences, debriefing failures, and sharing information regularly, they'd become excited about the jobs they were doing. They were becoming aware of the difference they were making to each other, and to the company, and were absolutely focused on developing their skills to become full contributing members of the organization.

Without our prompting, they expressed a genuine desire to serve the organization that employed them.

If we lived in tribe, this high level of participation and service would come to us naturally. There would also be an immediate feedback loop, showing us how our actions impact our tribe. We wouldn't have to go out looking for that information; we'd be immersed in it. The tribe would only exist because each of us serves it, creates it, loves it, and in return is held by it.

This inherent awareness of the interconnectedness that shapes our tribal values was reflected by Chief Seattle, nearly 150 years ago, when he said:

"All things are connected like blood which unites one family...
Man did not weave the web of life; he is merely a strand in it.
Whatever he does to the web, he does to himself."

The following quote, by Albert Schweitzer, beautifully explains service:

"I don't know what your destiny will be, but one thing I know: the only ones among you who will really be happy are those who have sought and found how to serve."

Serve and you will be fulfilled; love and you will experience love; risk and you will know the edges of your capacity; feel your own pain and you will have compassion for all others around you, and gain the power of forgiveness.

Once we've developed our capacities of belonging, recognition, ritual, and education, we're inevitably led to the next big question: "My life is in service to what?" To use a metaphor, what good is it to develop a beautiful musical instrument if it's never played! Like members of an orchestra, when we bring ourselves to our human tribe and practice the skills of participation, we blend our sounds with our partners, our children, our fellow community members, to form a sound far richer than any of us could create alone. The sound we create as one uplifts our hearts and informs our souls of the mystery.

Our friend Hal Bennett, who is also an author, speaks to young writers at bookstore presentations. He instructs these aspiring authors to look around them at all the books on the shelves. And then he asks the question, "What will you write about? Hasn't everything been said, not once but a million times? There is nothing new under the sun. Except for one thing: you! There has never been another voice like yours. If you truly tell your own life experience and in your own voice, you will bring a brand new perspective to any subject under the sun. And when you do that, you just might make it possible for others to hear it for the first time—even though it has been said a million times before!"

WE NEED A MAP

A number of years ago we were traveling with a group in Thailand. During one of our free days, some of us were drawn to crowds of families standing at the gateway to a temple. These were the families of Initiates. They had come to say good-bye to their sons, to witness the ritual that would mark a major passage in the boys' lives. They would be leaving a familiar way of life and would now be dedicating themselves to the spiritual life. About a dozen Initiates were gathered, ages eleven to eighteen. Today, they would leave behind their worldly clothing and shave their heads publicly, symbolizing their renunciation of the everyday world. They would drape their bodies with the monks' robes, a symbol of the brotherhood they were joining.

A bittersweet mixture of pride and loss was seen in the faces of family members, while anxiety, hope, and determination were present in the faces of the Initiates. Horns blew, offerings were burned, prayers and chants were sung as the boys completed the public rites and stepped into this spiritual brotherhood. Today they began a life of devotion and service.

We watched, transfixed. Here we were, a group of Westerners who had set out that day to go shopping in Bangkok. But here at the entrance to the temple we watched in awe, seeing something most of us would never experience in our sophisticated Western lives. As we imagined the lives these young men were entering, we felt our own longing to have such clear and meaningful blueprints for living, and to be as connected to what we were serving in our lives. We felt our yearning for a life infused with mindfulness, purpose and meaning.

When we fully give ourselves to a purpose, backed by perseverance and commitment, our lives have a direction. Many of us, however, cling to outdated or meager purposes. We may have big dreams, yet over and over again we refuse to take the actions that would fulfill that vision. With tribal values at the forefront of our lives, our choices become easier, clearer, and our lives more exciting and more meaningful.

LOOK, WE'RE HAVING AN IMPACT!

As children, we all experienced a time when we believed that reality was made up of only that which we could see with our two eyes, or otherwise detect with our five senses. One of my (Carole) memories of being a young child takes me back to a time when my parents bought a new refrigerator. It came in a huge cardboard box, and I remember playing in this box, indeed, creating a whole universe in that little space. I marched around in front of my parents and their guests, hidden inside my box. I remember being absolutely sure that they could not see me, because I could not see them seeing me. They played along with the game, saying things like, "Where's Carole? Where could she have gone?" I gleefully threw the box off my head and cried, "Here I am! Here I am!" I was certain they could not see me until that moment.

As adults, too many of us are like the child inside the box, thinking that we have no impact because we can make ourselves relatively invisible. But the fact remains that we are always having an impact, and are always being affected by those around us.

We need to be accountable for our impact, whatever that impact may be. We need to come out of our boxes. We need to commit ourselves to this practice in the most direct and simple ways. That might mean taking responsibility for the things we say or don't say at work. It might mean honestly telling our loved ones what effect they are having on us, or opening ourselves to feel the effect we are having on another person. Practicing accountability also means seeing that even the smallest act of reaching out makes a huge difference, to ourselves and others.

When we live from a tribal consciousness, we understand that each of our actions is woven into the tapestry of the entire community. From this level of awareness we understand that we must be responsible for sharing our gifts, and taking actions that serve.

Without the guidance provided by our awareness of our tribe, it is easy for us to withdraw when our participation is needed. Often our commitment to our participation is based on how we feel, as opposed to what will serve, or what will contribute. Without this vital awareness of our impact on others, it becomes easy to trash and pollute the earth, deliver late on our promises, or withhold compliments. If we don't awaken to the tribal experience and to our influence in the world, we get further from everyone—and most tragically, from ourselves.

AGREEMENTS: THE FOUNDATION

One evening we had a meeting with two women surgeons who were in practice together. They came to us wanting help with their business partnership. Their business was doing well, but they had concerns about staff relationships, and how things would progress as their practice expanded. They talked about how much they respected each other and enjoyed being partners. What we noticed was that they hadn't created a tribe with each other, or their staff.

During the session we had asked them the following questions:

- What is the purpose of your partnership?
- How often do you meet to discuss what is working and not working in your business partnership?
- How do you handle conflicts that arise? What mechanisms

do you use to communicate upsets or problems to each other?
- What agreements does your partnership operates under?
- What actions do you take to support those agreements?
- Why did you come together as business partners? What, if any, vows did you make to each other? What actions do you take to support those vows?

The two women were genuinely surprised! They realized that they had focused a lot of attention on creating legal and financial agreements with each other, but had never had any discussions that would assist them in creating the kind of tribe they both wanted.

Our couples-work frequently reveals such blind spots. It's always enlightening to send a couple off to separately make lists of the vows they think they made to each other. We also ask them to list the assumptions and agreements of their relationship. Almost without fail, they come back with very different lists! They then begin to see that the differing assumptions are the reason for so many of the mixed messages, for so much of the confusion and pain they have been living with. For any relationship to grow and thrive, the vows we take must become the values our actions must continuously serve.

We often try to imagine how a Hmong villager would counsel modern couples to help them build relationships from a foundation of service. We can picture the Hmong counselor telling these couples to look around them, to take careful note of what they see happening in the village. The villager might suggest they ask what is their purpose for their relationship, and what agreements they should make to support it. Their counselor might emphasize the need for actions that build trust. There would be a powerful underlying message—that if the couple's relationship was to succeed, they would have to understand that they both needed each other's best efforts and greatest gifts.

In tribal living we would know that not showing up could mean that an entire garden dies and a lot of people go hungry. Our unwillingness to share what we learn about medicine and herbal remedies could severely affect the health of the clan. Today we have lost touch with this basic human understanding. We honor commitments to our partners if it happens to be convenient, and then we wonder why our relationships aren't more intimate; we're surprised when people in our lives are less than trustworthy. We seem to know so little about creating and honoring agreements that establish a strong foundation for those times when we need to pull together. We haven't lived in the ongoing presence of a tribal "us," and so we end up failing in business, ending our marriages, or suffering alone. We lack the values, the skills, and the daily practices that could have carried us through the hard times.

A WOMAN'S DANCE

We need a model for participating in life that can bring each person, as well as the tribe, into accord with who we are, at the deepest levels of our humanity. We serve the tribe and we touch our own souls. Here is one woman's account of such a moment:

HOW STRANGE to find myself in this group," I thought on the first night. I had agreed to come to the workshop because it was important to my youngest son David that I be there; but on a deeper level I knew I was there to work through my own unresolved material, to cross a threshold I had never crossed early in my life—the experience of truly valuing myself as a woman and giving myself permission to become that woman in the presence of others, including my son and daughter. I felt like I was risking the alienation of my children—so much about me and my life I had kept hidden from them. Somehow I knew that Sunday morning it was time for me to remove the constraints of my own making, be vulnerable in public, in the presence of my children, in the presence of the tribe of men and women who were gathered.

I was called into the center of the room to dance in front of the entire tribe—to dance the woman's dance; the dance of a woman who wanted to be recognized and valued. I closed my eyes and felt all the places inside that weren't someone's mother, or someone's daughter. I felt the woman that I am, and felt her movements begin to dance my body. As I opened my eyes, I saw other women joining me, the others who knew themselves truly as women. I saw the tears streaming down some of the women's faces, tears of recognition. We danced the women's dance together. From behind me one woman put her arms around me and led me in the dance, letting me move as she moved, until I was connected to her energy, her ability to feel and to nurture and to love, and until all the loving places in my own heart slowly began to open. I saw my children looking on, seeing the woman I am dancing through their mother's body, and felt how little they actually knew of me before this moment.

The men joined in, forming their own circle around us, and we could feel how important it is for women to be witnessed by men as something other than the roles we play as mother or daughter. The men were then called into the circle with each other, to feel the strength of each other's shoulders on either side of them, to recognize how much goes unsaid between men, to witness the vulnerability of being a man. As I stood in the circle of women, listening to the men, and seeing how beautiful they were with each other, I felt us come together as one tribe. I felt the courage inside me that had begun this circle, the love that I feel for my children, and my soul calling me forward that day, paving the way for my transformation. I have rarely felt such humanity as was present that day. I knew I had crossed the threshold that I had been reaching for; I would no longer hold myself separate from my children, and from the people I love.

In the Hmong village there would be no reason to keep one's wisdom, beauty, pain, discoveries, or challenges hidden away. To do so wouldn't serve anyone. With the tribe's well-being and enrichment as the guiding star, generous, compassionate action is called for—each individual's participation vital to the well-being of the entire tribe.

WHAT KIND OF PERSON DO YOU WANT TO BE?

One summer I (Jodi) spent some time wandering around Tibet, in the capitol city of Lhasa. The main temple where people go to pray in the city is called "The Jokang," and around it is a cobblestone marketplace called "The Barkor." Next to tea stands there are stalls selling exotic spices, children's clothing, temple incense, and huge chunks of yellow yak butter. The market teems with life. On a single street corner there are businessmen, monks, nuns, beggars, babies, military police, and school children.

One afternoon, I was having some tea and watching the day go by. Surrounded by all this bustling activity, I saw a man lying down on the cobblestone walkway. I watched him stand up, take one step to his left, and lie down again. I realized he was doing full body prostrations. He was literally doing a prostration on each section of the cobblestone. He never looked up. He simply continued to lay himself down in surrender, over and over again. Through the course of the days I was in Lhasa, I saw this man in the market place every afternoon—doing his practice, carefully stepping one foot over to his left, then again giving this practice every bit of strength and energy he had. Determination was chiseled across his brow, his exhaustion level rising with each step, yet he continued for up to four hours each day.

As I watched him, I could feel what this man knew in his body and with every fiber of his being about service and devotion. I was so moved by him. It mattered not to me what he was bowing to, but simply that he was bowing, that he would give every ounce of his being as an act of love to whatever he prayed for, that he would do it right out in the middle of the market place, for all the world to witness. For me, he embodied devotion as I had never seen before. I spent a lot of time that trip asking myself the questions, "What do I serve?" What do I bow to?"

We have to begin asking these questions. We have to set up purposeful action in service to the tribes we are a part of and love. To participate as tribe members we need to honor who and what we are, and create the tribal reality of which we want to be a part.

PLAYING THE PART FOR WHICH YOU WERE CAST

Once we open up and dedicate ourselves to service in any arena of our lives, we realize that we are not alone. We are part of a tribe, a greater collective. We don't have to be all things to all people. We don't have to be famous, rich, talented or beautiful. When we live in tribe we understand that the entire group, all of us, are of one fabric, one soul. We come to recognize the tribe as an expression of wholeness.

I (Carole) have a friend who went to his twenty-fifth high school reunion. In high school he had been a loner. He'd been the kind of kid who stood on the outside looking in. He called me after the reunion dinner and said that nothing had changed in all those twenty-five years. The popular ones gathered at the center of the room, in a circle, and the same ones who had been on the outside were still standing on the outside. But what had changed was his re- lationship to it. He said that in surveying the scene he realized that it takes the inside to create an outside, and that the outer ones served the inner circle. He saw that one couldn't exist without the other. Together they were whole, each playing the part they knew so well. He felt appreciation and love for the majesty of his role, realized that being an outer observer was what he liked and what he did best. He no longer felt he was inadequate for not playing an inside role.

It's an enormous relief to realize that we don't have to be anything other than who we are. Life needs us all. Everything we are, all that we experience, all that we feel, serves life when it we bring it with balance and love. Where would we be without high notes and low notes, without the positive and negative poles of a magnet, without negative numbers as well as positive ones?

Just as in the world at large, the wholeness of a tribe depends on diversity. In some tribes there are dreamers who dream for the collective. There are other members who have children, who hunt, who are teachers of the young, who heal, who are caretakers, or who need caretaking. Our families and work places generally function the same way. We each hold a balance for the other. The black sheep of the family propagates new ideas, shakes up the group through conflict or bewilderment. The good children of the same family are the glue that maintains the established values.

Joseph Campbell once noted that in every marriage there are three "members" to be considered and cared for—you, your spouse, and the relationship. The relationship is like a person itself, requiring care in the same way your spouse and you require it. And the relationship has a life of its own, expressing aspects of you and your spouse that you could not express without it. The same might be said for the tribe. To see the tribe as a living, breathing entity, expressing everything that its members bring to it, is to grasp the significance of what it means to be human. We are all the totality of everything that gets expressed through this third member we call the tribe.

It can be useful to think of ourselves as one portion of a very large body, and to then ask ourselves, "What part of that body am I? Is my function to eliminate, or to transport? Am I the eyes or ears or liver?" When we forget that we all hold different parts of life for each other we reject our differences, trying to turn ourselves into something we are not, or worse, trying to hammer everything outside us into our own image.

A wondrous thing happens when we live as if everyone's life is in service to the collective. We can see our roles change with the passage of time, and we can see how our place at the wheel of life changes. For example, I (Carole) watch my son's pride when he, now five years old, returns after summer vacation to his three-, four-, and five-year-old's Montessori class. He is called upon, simply through his place in this tribe, to teach the younger, incoming members. These younger ones have never been there before. They don't know what to expect. But Zach has been there. He knows. He can support them, serve them, in their passage to their new place in this classroom. As he observes these new students coming in, Zach becomes intuitively aware that he has been where they are now, and he himself has moved on. And that's important: each member being able to experience himself within the continuity of the tribe.

We don't suggest that each member of the tribe must act a certain way. What we do advocate is that each member of a tribe be purposeful, acting in service to the larger tribe, humanity itself. This act of service can take many forms. We might use the metaphor of baking a cake, where we can see that any single ingredient by itself can be unappetizing, but must be included or we don't end up with a cake. Our tribe members are like that, each one serving in a unique and necessary way. Each and every one of us brings far more to the mix than we can even imagine. It's easy to miss what we contribute because we sometimes focus on what we are *not* instead of what we are.

POTENTIAL IS NOT FULFILLMENT

When I (Carole) was a little girl I wanted to learn to play the piano. I had no sense of what that would take. I had music in my heart, and I imagined that I could sit at the piano and music would pour through my soul to the keys, filling the room with what I heard in my heart. In my five-year-old fashion I begged my parents to buy me a piano. And oh, how I kept it up! Then, one day, my mother said that if I understood what it would take—a lot of lessons and hard work—she would get me a piano, but once I started, she would never let me stop. I agreed.

I will never forget the day the piano arrived. It was on my sixth birthday. I came home from school and there it stood in the living room! I walked over to it, lifted up the keyboard cover, sat down on the bench, and placed my hands on the keys. Regardless of my mother's warnings, I still imagined that I would instantly be able to play the music in my heart. What issued from the keys was the most hideous sound! I was appalled. Devastated. My mother gently reminded me that I would need many lessons before I was able to make the sounds I longed to hear. It did indeed take many years.

The lesson here is that it is not enough to simply recognize our potential. We may have something in our souls that we long to express and contribute. But longing and desire are not enough. We must also develop the skills to bring it forth, and develop relationships with a tribe to bring it into. To love is not enough; we must offer our love in service if we are to fully experience it and know our true meaning and purpose.

BEING USED WELL

Often, we run into people who are reluctant to dedicate themselves to service. "I'm afraid of being used," they say. We have a different perspective. We would hope that, at the end of our lives, any one of us would be able to look back and feel that we had been well-used by the tribe. In this way, we would have served, made a difference, learned a tremendous amount—we would have been able to feel our lives had purpose. But first we need to consciously ask, "What kind of a tribe do I want to belong to, and what kind of a person do I want to be within it?" These are powerful questions, leading us to ask other questions about our potentials. How might we make contributions that allow us to fully realize who we are, not just in terms of who we are when we are alone, but who we are in relationship to everything beyond ourselves?

DEVOTION

We know what it is to be devoted deeply enough to a child that we rock them through the long, seemingly endless nights of illness, only to have to go to work early the next day. We know what it is to be so passionately devoted to the building of a company that we sacrifice our hobbies, our free time, and even our intimate relationships to the struggles of its creation. We know what it is to plant a garden and lovingly devote ourselves to the watering of those new shoots through the hot summer days.

Devotion is the care and feeding of that which you have chosen to serve. It's an act of service in itself, and it is an act of love.

What we get for devotion is the experience of creating and loving something. Will we, in our longing, be devoted to tribe? What would be different if as we went to our jobs every day, we experienced ourselves connecting with our tribe—our lives devoted to it because we fully believed in everything it stood for? How would our actions be different if we were practicing devotion at that level?

THE TRIBE SERVES LIFE

Once when we were trekking in Thailand we stayed in a Karen village, where I (Carole) met and made friends with a beautiful fourteen-year-old girl. During the course of the day we played together, miming, walking, just being with each other. She spoke no English, and for most of the day my interpreter was gone. Toward the end of the day, we were joined by my interpreter. My friend shyly left the village hut we had been sitting in, and I asked the interpreter where she had gone.

He answered, "She will be right back. There is something very important that she wants you to see."

When my young friend returned she was carrying a stunningly beautiful piece of woven fabric. It was so intricate, full of vibrant deep reds, blues, and indigos.

As she held it out for me to see, my interpreter told me, "She has been weaving this for many years. Each day, as she sits down to her weaving, she sings her prayers and dreams, weaving them into the cloth." He paused before going on, then said, "It is her marriage dress. Until she is married she will always wear the white cloth she is in now."

Her once white cotton dress was so stained by the earth and the smoke of the cooking fires I hadn't really been aware of it. But as I saw the contrast between the dress she wore and the one she was weaving, I looked around and indeed, all the young girls wore exactly the same dingy white cotton garb.

"How do they choose their mates?" I asked my interpreter. He said, "Whenever someone of the same tribe dies, all of the neighboring villages that belong to that tribe gather. They have the funeral, they grieve, they dance, tell stories, and all the young men and women who are of an age to marry meet and choose a mate. They all must wait patiently until someone dies. Then, they can marry! Her fabric has been complete and she has been waiting for a funeral for two years now."

I was so moved by the beauty and symmetry of this system, that in the shadow of death, new families and new lives would come into being. And as this young girl sat weaving the cloth, she was surrounded by women who knew how to create a garment such as this, who could answer her questions when she felt like giving up, or made a mistake in her weaving. She sat in the presence of men and women who had met their mates this way, who had witnessed death and birth in the marriage cycle over and over again. Within this tribal context, the young woman could weave the threads of hope for her future as a woman.

SERVICE IS CARING IN ACTION

Service is caring in action. Caring, wanting, desiring—these can't be passive processes. They have to be coupled with an action in order to build and strengthen what we care about.

Our challenge today is that, unlike the young people in the Karen village, we don't yet have a feeling of belonging, enough to overcome our resistance. If we don't feel we belong, then of course service feels like we're giving up something, some obligation to be avoided at all costs. But unless we're willing to serve, we'll never have any kind of relationship, family, or community to which we *can* belong.

Our question is whether we're willing to feel how much we care, how deeply we want to connect, how much we want to be part of something larger than ourselves. If we're willing to care and to do something from that caring, then without having to be extraordinary, without having to be anything more than we are, we'll find ways to make a difference. We'll find the courage to risk offering ourselves in service, and see what our caring can create.

Voices Of The Tribe

Twenty years ago I passed the age of thirty without challenging the notion that people over thirty can't be trusted. I thought young, dressed young, played young, acted young. I hadn't noticed how exhausting it had become. As we stood in the tribal circle I was overcome with the realization that I was an elder. It was the first time that I had ever acknowledged that, or felt the truth of eldership's contribution. I took my place as my age for the first time that day. As the burden of being eternally young eases, the understanding and assurance that I possess a wisdom to be honored and to be shared takes its place. This is powerfully validating. I am seeing the passage of time as a friend . . . bringing me to a life that is fuller, more trustworthy (and a whole lot easier) than trying to perpetuate the myth that I am still a young warrior. Power has given way to service.

—Ralph Hoar

This voice is a reflection on service from a woman who was helping during a Women's Gathering:

> *One night we had a sweat lodge. I stood by the little doorway, and as the women crawled out, I helped them get up. I felt very protective of them. I tried to make sure each woman was okay, and would steady them if they needed it. It felt so precious supporting them; I still feel tender whenever I think about it.*
>
> *Many of them didn't want or need support. One woman in particular just shot past me, saying she was fine. Later she talked about how lonely she felt because in her life she never asked for help and avoided any when offered.*
>
> *I knew that part of myself, usually so strong like that, and that all the women in my family are so afraid of burdening someone else that they'll do it all by themselves. I started to feel so sad about the times my mother or my sisters didn't tell me they were sick until after the crisis was over. And I had to laugh at how many times I've done exactly the same thing.*
>
> *I wondered when was the last time I'd had a chance to really support my family, and show them how much I loved them with a simple touch. And I started to understand why it felt so healing to me when those wet women, my sisters for that week at least, let themselves lean on me.*
>
> —Virginia M. Fleming

8

THE SIXTH VALUE: TRUST AND FAITH

To know that what is impenetrable to us really exists,
manifesting itself as the highest wisdom and the most radi-
ant beauty, which our dull facilities can comprehend only
in the most primitive forms—this knowledge, this feeling,
is at the center of all true religiousness. In this sense, and
in this sense only, I belong to the ranks of the devoutly
religious men.

—*Albert Einstein*

Today, like every other day, we wake up empty and frightened. Don't open the door to the study and begin reading.
Take down a musical instrument.

Let the beauty we love be what we do.

There are hundreds of ways to kneel and kiss the ground.

—*Rumi*

A COUPLE OF YEARS AGO, Carole and I (Jodi) were driving
through Rocky Mountain National Park. I had never been
to the Rocky Mountains before, and I really wanted to see
them. It was very foggy, and as we wound higher and higher up the
passes, it got so foggy that we couldn't even see the car in front of us.
We decided to pull over for a while to wait for the traffic to pass. We
just sat there, enveloped by fog, unable to see anything. My trip to
the mountains was turning out to be pretty disappointing.

Then slowly, almost miraculously, the clouds gently parted, and there in all of their glory and majesty were the Rocky Mountains, rising out of the mists! We had only a few minutes before the clouds rolled back in and we were again immersed, unable to see the mountains—but knowing absolutely that they were there. Teary-eyed, I looked over at Carole and said, "This is how life works, isn't it?" The majesty of the mountains is always present; it's only the limits of our own vision, our inability to see through the fog, that prevents us from seeing them.

We know there are forces that we cannot see, but which nevertheless influence the course of our lives. The life force itself is this way. We see evidence of its existence all around us, animating all living things; but the force itself, the life spirit, is invisible. Nowhere is this truth more dramatically manifested for us than when we witness a birth or a person's death. Through the joining of an egg and sperm, suddenly a new life comes into being! As the physical body ceases to function, the life force departs. We can witness it, stand in its presence, even feel it, but it is forever a mystery of an unseen reality.

Early tribal man's daily life always included honoring his relationship with this invisible world. He never lost touch with it, and never could, because in some small way every part of his visible world was connected to it. This ability to keep us connected us to the mystery of life is perhaps one of the most wondrous functions of tribe.

In his book *Memories, Dreams, Reflections*, Carl Jung tells of visiting and speaking with the Taos Indians, in New Mexico. Sitting on the highest roof of the pueblo, one of his hosts explains, "We are a people who live on the roof of the world; we are the sons of Father Sun, and with our religion we daily help our father to go across the sky. We do this not only for ourselves, but for the whole world. If we were to cease practicing our religion, in ten years the sun would no longer rise. Then it would be night forever."[1]

Humans throughout history have used rituals to celebrate the passages of the seasons, the cycles of the moon, birthing, growing, changing, and death. They have used them for calling the spirits and accessing the invisible realms to aid and nurture human endeavor. Without the rituals that connect human life to the ongoing flow of the natural world, we perhaps forget our life purpose, that which gives us our sense of meaning.

Jung reflected on the quiet, centered dignity that he observed in these people of the Taos tribe. He said of them, "It springs from his being a son of the sun; his life is cosmologically meaningful, for he helps the father and preserver of all life in his daily rise and descent."[2]

Today we call beliefs such as those of the Taos Indians "primitive," yet at the core of our own instincts is this *knowing* that we are just as wedded to the natural forces. When we spend time in nature, perhaps sleeping out under the stars, we feel the beauty of participating in life. Part of the value of tribe is to make known, once again, the unknowable. Tribe provides ways for people to enter and remember what many people would claim as their birthright: to truly feel part of life's unfolding mystery. To feel one's breath as part of life's breath, to be connected on a more essential level. To know one's life as part of something much vaster than can be seen with ordinary eyes.

At the heart of many tribal rituals, including those which we hope this book will awaken, is the intention to express man's awareness of how his life is linked with the *great round,* to all that is. Jung spoke of these rituals as responses to God. He said that the person who feels connected in this way "feels capable of formulating valid replies to the overpowering influence of God, and that he can render back something which is essential even to God." This capacity "induces pride, for it raises the human individual to the dignity of a metaphysical factor."[3]

When we participate in tribe we are more likely to experience, if only for a moment, this *other sight,* the vision required to perceive what is not apparent to our ordinary eyes. Through tribal participation we begin to understand that something much deeper, fuller, and richer than what our rational minds can grasp moves our lives, and connects us with all there is. And with that recognition, ordinary life begins to take on new dimensions.

DREAMS CAN BUILD A BRIDGE

In *Man And His Symbols* Jung said, "A symbol is a visible statement of an invisible reality."[4]

One way to the vast resources of what we can't see is through the symbolic world, the world of our images and dreams. The unconscious speaks to us through symbolic language. Hidden in the expanse of our unconscious is a wealth of capacity, usually unexplored. Our dreams are the gateway to hidden talents, unknown feelings, options for healing and balance, and much more. They can inform us, communicate to us, and help us adjust our attitudes. Within our dreams we can even find the answers to unfathomable questions.

At one point in my life I (Carole) was struggling with the decision of whether to leave my employment with a personal growth and development company. I had begun to question the integrity of the company I worked for. I was also at issue with what was being taught, and how. But I was unsure whether or not I would be a capable teacher on my own. I was torn in myself. So, I asked for a dream to assist me, and this is the one I received:

I am walking down the street barefoot, carrying a pair of athletic shoes that my employer had given me. I am looking for a trash can to dispose of the shoes because, even though they had served me well, the soles were coming off. Just then my boss comes up to me and says, "Don't throw those shoes away. I gave those to you. They are still good."

I thank him for the shoes but let him know that they had taken me as far as they could. Even though I will have to go barefoot for a while, I know that I will, in time, find my own shoes that will take me where I must go.

This dream was direct. It let me know that my concern about the "sole" or "soul" of the company was not just a passing concern. It also informed me that the very foundation of the kind of teaching I was doing might not be congruent with my deeper nature. If I left, I would be exposed and vulnerable, but I was likely to find my own capacity, my foundation, and my teaching. The dream also let me know that I would be okay. I would find my new shoes.

That dream helped me through the first two years of starting my own teaching work. It was a reminder to me that it was okay that I didn't know what to do, or what decisions to make. And after a while, what the dream told me did come to pass. I had found my own shoes!

As this dream shows, the symbolic language of the unconscious can be our bridge to what is usually unknowable. Dreams are just one way we can get in touch with this aspect of our being. We can also reach it through meditation, prayer, art, music, dance and other forms of deep personal expression.

TOUCHING THE INVISIBLE

Making the decision to trust an invisible source of knowledge can be difficult, particularly if we only trust what we can see and understand, or if we think there is nothing bigger than ourselves. When we trust only what we know, we have only our will and our ego to fall back on, and that is when we get the feeling that we are adrift in the boundless sea of life. If I trust that there are forces greater than myself that I can call upon, then I can be in partnership with something informing, something whole. To partner with the unconscious forces that guide our lives, we must practice trusting what can't be readily seen.

One of the more familiar ways of trusting what can't be seen is prayer. Anyone can pray, anywhere, anytime—and we often do! Prayer is a petitioning, a call to source, to God, and then opening ourselves so that something larger and wiser might answer. As Thomas Merton described it, "One opens the inner doors of one's heart to the infinite silences of spirit, out of whose abysses love wells up without fail and gives itself to all."[5]

There are also many stories and myths about opening the unseen world. It is said that in ancient Hawaiian tribal culture, a boy would go out with his grandfather just before the boy's awakening into puberty, and together they would plant a banana tree. As they did the planting, the grandfather would pray aloud for the boy's and the tree's health and prosperity, asking that they might both flourish and bear fruit.

Just as the banana tree bore its first fruit, the boy would come into his puberty, the onset of his own phallic power. What a beautiful ritual. What a beautiful link to life, to the earth! The boy learns about nurturing his own development as he nurtures and tends his tree. He learns about his own power, and the desire to offer back the power as sustenance, food and support for his tribe. He is held at that moment in the trust of his grandfather, who knows the cycle that his grandson is entering.

This story tells us that tribal rituals mirror the mystery back to its members. The tribe passes those rites, rituals, ceremonies and stories from generation to generation to preserve their invisible connection. The rituals make visible what we cannot see. They clothe the sacred realms, allowing us to feel and see the presence of the vast mountains beyond the mist.

CRISIS AS OPPORTUNITY

In our lifetimes we have seen many great crises in the world, ranging from new strains of viruses that threaten the lives of millions, to increases in crime and unemployment, to devastating earthquakes, fires, and storms. In every case, there are thousands of people whose lives are touched by these disasters, and who find that during times of crisis they reach for trust and faith.

In crisis, some people even experience powerful openings to positive change in their lives. When people were confronted with these great natural forces, they saw that they had no choice but to surrender. In surrendering, they discovered truths that opened them up to life, that reconnected them with the unseen.

For the most part, we do not often have such deep, unyielding faith. We don't live every day greeting each moment of life as a blessing, gifted to us so we might develop, learn, and serve. Our lives change radically when we choose to live with this kind of belief. But we lose our connection, again and again, unless we live with the tribal practices that naturally link us to this trust.

A STORY OF SURRENDER

THE DAY I found out I was HIV positive was and still is one of the most memorable days in my life. I had just celebrated my thirty-first birthday when I got a call from a woman at the Irwin Memorial Blood Bank. She said she had been trying to get hold of me for a few weeks, but hadn't wanted to leave a message on the answering machine. At that moment my heart sank to my belly. She said it was against their policy to disclose why she was calling, but my last donation had been tested, and they had found something. She asked if I could come for an appointment in the next few hours. Those few hours waiting at home were the worst of my life.

I remember sitting on my bed trying to meditate, to calm myself, feeling scared, frantic and alone. I was scared that I would die. I was a white, well-educated, middle-class woman. People like me didn't get AIDS. It had not seemed necessary to worry about it, or even to educate myself about it.

In the weeks after discovering that I was HIV positive, I went about my life mechanically. I was a consultant, seeing three or four clients on-site every day. When I was in my car driving from one client to the next it would hit me; I would sob while I was driving, arrive at my client's and get myself together enough to function. While I was at my client's site, I would forget completely about being HIV positive and get totally immersed in my work. Then I would get back in my car and sob. There would be times when I could actually forget that I was HIV positive. But I was a completely different person now. I blamed only myself for being HIV positive, not the man who infected me. I felt guilt and shame, and my lifetime suspicion that I was a truly unworthy person was confirmed by this disease. So those times that I forgot I was HIV positive, or even felt some joy, seemed wrong or unreal to me.

When I think about where I was then and the person I have become now, it seems to me that the transformation has been slow and gradual. But there are some very specific things I remember that were like quantum leaps in my consciousness and healing. My foundation and supporting structure were always and still are: having a gifted therapist, an incredibly talented, caring, and aggressive doctor, and a close relationship with my family. More recently I developed a circle of friends, a tribe, who love and care for me.

The first leap was when I realized that "healing" didn't necessarily mean "curing the disease." I had to shift to taking good care of myself. In the New Testament, Christ commands us to "Love thy neighbor as thyself," and I had never had problems with the *love thy neighbor* bit. However, I had a heck of a time with the *love thyself* part. What happened when I started to be caring and loving to myself was that I started to enjoy my life. I had always wanted to learn ballroom dancing, so I took dance lessons. I found a horse to ride and rediscovered that incredible bond a woman can develop with her horse. One day while driving down the freeway I realized how joyful my life was, and I started to cry. Why had it taken a life-threatening disease for me to finally feel some joy in my life?

In the face of a life threatening illness, I started asking myself, "What do I want right now, in this instance?" What an incredible gift! Imagine if you were to do that for a week, how you would feel and what your life would be like. I don't mean that I suddenly became decadent and indulgent. On the contrary! How it shifted my life was that I realized that if I was on my death bed I probably wouldn't regret that I had been five pounds overweight. More likely I would regret that I hadn't spent more time in cafes sipping coffee in the sunshine!

I started to ask myself, "What if I were to begin looking at my life as if it were a wonderful opportunity to solve a puzzle?" I started to look with wonder at the process that was happening in my body. I began to lose the judgment I had about it or to even have a preference about what was happening to it. I realized that what was happening to me was a sacred process, no matter what the outcome. Lucky to be HIV positive? It was actually a shock to have that surface in my consciousness—how could that possibly be?

As I look back, and reflect on who I am today, I can only be grateful for I know I would definitely not be who I am if I had not become HIV positive. I realized that if I was given a chance to go back in time and change that critical moment when I became infected, I would not change a thing.

This woman, a member of our tribe, found that such a devastating disease opened up her life to immense resource and opportunity. As she shared her experiences with our tribe, people who were not facing such devastation also began to take stock of their lives, ask similar questions, and come to new realizations.

EXPERIENCING WHAT CANNOT BE SEEN

We have all had moments where we can feel the presence of unseen forces moving like a river through our lives. Those moments are often the ones that we remember during times of great challenge, or strife. A number of years ago, a friend of mine (Jodi) spent some time on retreat in the desert. Fred had been a successful stockbroker with a large New York firm, and it was quite unusual for him to be away from the phone for any period of time. He spent most of the retreat in meditation, looking across a great vista to a beautiful sacred mountain.

Over a series of days, Fred got quieter and quieter within himself. The mountain became an important symbol to him, reflecting something solid, a foundation, continuity and timelessness. About four months later, after returning to New York from the desert, the stock market crash of 1987 occurred, causing him, his clients, and his family to lose a great deal of money—at a time when he was engaged to be married. When I called to see how he was doing, all he could say was, "Thank God for the mountain. The mountain is always there no matter what comes to pass. I've been remembering it, and it has been getting me through this horrible time."

It was not the mountain itself that gave him this strength, of course, but something invisible and ineffable which somehow communicated to him through the symbol of *mountain*, a symbol which he had internalized and now carried within him. Throughout the centuries human beings have drawn much resource and inspiration from the symbolic realm. We need to remember to stay open to what cannot be seen, learning to build a bridge between our conscious and unconscious minds.

STAYING OPEN TO LIFE

To participate fully in life requires the same trust and openness with which we birthed into life. Out of this trust and participation there can ultimately emerge a deep sense of unconditional love. Alice has always been a role model for me (Carole) of what it takes to trust and have unconditional love. She lived so much from her deep trust in life that she would rarely judge or quantify life. The thought of deciding that something was good or bad, right or wrong, was simply outside her awareness.

Alice lived each day as if it were her responsibility to participate completely in whatever showed up. She truly believed that if she felt something was "not quite right with life," she must be failing to understand what life was handing her. Like Joseph Campbell, who asked, "Who created this wondrous plot of my life?," Alice believed with the deepest faith that life has a way of providing exactly what is needed for our growth and development. My favorite story about what it was like to be around Alice's unconditional acceptance and love is this:

In her seventies Alice began to lose her eyesight to cataracts. I had moved to San Francisco, and decided that I wanted her to have the opportunity to see some of the things she soon might not be able to see. She flew out, and for a week we visited the majestic redwoods, the ocean, beautiful gardens, and Fisherman's Wharf. And one day, half-jokingly, I made a reference to Disneyland. Alice looked at me and asked, "What's Disneyland?"

So I described the theme park, the food, the rides, the fantasies, and I told her, "There is even a roller coaster that you can ride in the dark!" Alice asked, "What's a roller coaster?" She had never been on one. For all I could tell, she had never even seen one! Having grown up poor and black in the South, and then having gone to work as a maid when she was just a young woman, there had been little room for adventure in her life. I decided then and there that we would go to Disneyland. And we did!

We rented a wheelchair and took a stroll through the theme park. When she decided she was ready to go on a ride, Alice told me she wanted to go on "that roller coaster in the dark." I was terribly worried. I was afraid that Space Mountain would be too much for her, and would damage her in some way. I was also afraid that I hadn't explained it well, and that my failure to describe exactly what she was in for could put her in a very uncomfortable position. But Alice was determined, so we got in line at Space Mountain. I figured that we would have a few minutes in line for me to talk her out of it. At one point I said to her, "Alice . . . aren't you afraid?" She replied, "I haven't had the experience yet, so how can I be afraid?"

I realized then that Alice was simply not willing to project her fear into the future. Finally, when we got to the "chicken exit," the last chance to ditch out before the ride, I turned to her in exasperation and said, "See, you can't go on the ride if you . . . ." I had a whole shopping list of reasons why we should back out and take the chicken exit. But then I just blurted out, "Maybe you shouldn't go!" She turned to me and said, "Well, I don't have heart disease that I know of, and I am taller than you. And I sure ain't pregnant! So, let's go." And so, off we went on the ride.

During the ride I didn't hear a single sound from her. I couldn't even tell if she was breathing. At the end of the ride, it took two attendants to lift her onto her shaky legs. As we walked out the exit, I asked how she liked it. Her reply was beautiful. She said, "Well, I liked the parts where you go up, and I don't like the parts where you go down so good." She was unwilling to make a blanket judgment about liking it. There were parts she liked, and parts she didn't.

Alice has been a great teacher to me, showing me a truly open-handed approach to life. It is difficult indeed to have the deep, all-embracing faith in life that Alice reveals to us. But when we can we find this awareness within us, our lives can change completely.

Joseph Campbell once said that you could tell a lot about the values of a society by looking at the tallest buildings. Most of ours are monuments to communication, commerce, and finance. In the great cities these buildings tower above those that house human endeavors previously considered the heartbeat of a people. They dwarf our structures for the arts, music, the theater, religion—places where our humanity is explored and elevated. In the Western world, we are materially wealthy but spiritually bereft.

Life is already miraculous, just as it is. But having misplaced the maps that show us the path to that miracle, we become lost in the wilderness, disconnected from spirit and devotion. Then we try to fill the gap with more money, more power, more experiences. These substitutes leave us hungry, and more driven; we end up getting lost in a culture that is pushing for more extremes, more intensities of experience, and we grow hungrier still. But what if we lived in tribe and the way toward the unknown was pointed out to us? We wouldn't be lost. We would return to a simple appreciation of life, and a desire to gather resources within us instead of without.

THE TAO OF TRIBE

For many of us, our most precious moments occur when we find ourselves in life's deeper flows and streams. We can ask any group of people to describe these moments and they immediately use words such as harmony, wholeness, connection, clarity, awe, fulfillment. We know that when we are in touch with these states of consciousness, we are in contact with the deepest, most transcendent place of our hearts and souls.

As often as not, such experiences appear to be purely serendipitous. But no matter how disconnected or estranged from the invisible our lives might seem, we have as reference points the experiences when we feel ourselves to be part of what the Chinese philosopher Lao-tzu called *The Tao*:

The Tao[6]

We look and cannot see its face;
It is invisible.
We listen and cannot hear it sound;
It is inaudible.
We reach out to touch it but feel nothing;
It is formless.

—Lao-tzu, c. 604-531 B.C.

Sometimes our immersion in life provides us with not just an image, but feelings, smells, and sounds that together imprint an experience of the Tao within our consciousness. And once imprinted, it becomes a reminder, a sacred ritual. The following is just such an experience:

The Sacred River

It is so hot! About 120 degrees Fahrenheit. The only relief from the heat and the endless noise and congestion today, as with all days in Varanassi, is to go to the river. Since arriving in this holy Hindu city a few days earlier, Jodi and I (Carole) have spent most of each day and night out on a boat captained by a man we met earlier in our visit, who calls himself Moon. We have come to love being with Moon. He speaks some English, and is delighted to tell us what he knows and loves about his native land.

We go out into the middle of the river each day with Moon, bring the oars into the boat, and then drift on the river as we take in life. Everything happens here. The Sadhu (holy men) sit on the banks burning incense, chanting prayers, painting ancient markings of devotion upon their heads with white ash. The people come to the ghat (stairs) to bathe... men and boys together, women and girls. They gather here at the beginning and end of each day, to wash, gossip, chat, argue, present offerings to the river. Young children splash and play, laugh and swim.

After the bathing is finished each morning, the sari washers come, washing the beautiful multi-colored fabric in the river and then spreading them out on the banks to dry. The banks become covered in splendid color, like some extraordinary quilt. Wedding ritual boats make the age-old crossing to the far bank, drumming and chanting, signaling the special rituals about to take place. And always, there are the preparations for death.

Varanassi is one of the holiest places in India to be cremated. Many cremation fires burn day and night. On the river, the sacred Brahma bulls, too sacred to burn, float by, bloated in death; the carrion birds feed on their backs.

As night falls, more people come from town, purchasing their offerings by the side of the river—a small leaf and flower basket, small enough to be held in the palm of the hand, into which a single candle is placed. The offering is then invested with the purchaser's prayers and set adrift upon the river, until the river glows with the lights of a thousand or more prayers.

And on it goes, day after day, life upon the river. One day, we are sitting on the boat with Moon. He says, "I meet many Westerners, and they think it strange that we do everything upon the river, that we bathe here, drink here, wash our food and clothes here, offer the ashes of our dead, and the sacred, unburned bodies of the holy men, babies, and cows. But we do not think it strange. This is the great Mother Ganga. She is holy, and in her grace she receives everything, purifying and sanctifying it."

We are moved by his speech. We do have trouble imagining that people would wash their bodies, their clothes, their food, and cast their dead into the same river. But Moon is connected to something much deeper. As a matter of course in his life, he is connected to what is holy.

So many of us can intuit that some immutable force creates and sustains us, just as Moon perceived the great Mother Ganga sustains him. But we can't see this force with our everyday eyes; it escapes us. Perhaps it escapes us because we have lost direct contact with Nature herself.

I (Carole) recall when my mother died, being in the grip of great sorrow. A wise woman said to me, "Give your grief to the ocean. It is big enough to hold it. Let the ocean hold your grief in the same way that your body knows how to hold itself together." She was right, of course. Just those words were a reminder to me that I was not alone, that *I did not have to do it all myself.* Under pressure, it is easy to forget about the invisible forces that guide and sustain us. To be reminded of them is all we need to move on.

I (Carole) recall hearing Joseph Campbell ask how our bodies heal themselves. Of course, at every lecture there were always people with backgrounds in medicine or human psychophysiology who tried to answer in technical terms, going into long descriptions about the immune system and our body's various homeostatic mechanisms. Then Joseph would point out that we truly don't know. We can recite the mechanics and still not know. It is a mystery!

The mystery of birth alone should be enough to remind us of the powers of the unseen. There is a wonderful Buddhist saying that, if you put a single garland of leaves upon the seven seas, the chances of a sea turtle rising up and putting his head through the garland are better than the odds of a person being born! This story reminds us that life is a privilege, not to be taken for granted. It is amazing that we are even here.

I (Jodi) remember the night Carole's son, Zachary, was born. I was in Carole's room just hours after he arrived through an emergency C-section, following many hours of labor. Carole was resting, still under sedation from the surgery. I had planned to spend the night with her, just in case she needed anything. As I sat in the room, there was Zachary, less than four hours old and under six pounds, the tiniest being I had ever held in my arms. I felt overwhelmed with the delight of spending that evening holding him. He had such a difficult time getting born, and here was his introduction to life on earth!

Holding this tiny being in my arms was like holding life itself. There are no words to describe what I experienced. Barely a day old, he was so close to the mystery. I felt like I was holding the moon, the sun, the flowers, and the spring rain. His breath was the breath of life itself, his heartbeat the heartbeat of the earth, his openness as vast as the sky, his newness as hopeful as a glorious sunrise. As I sat with him that night and into the next morning, I knew I had come into the world this same way. We all do, of course. This is what the Sufis mean when they say we are all born in a state of "essence." Somehow, through the process of living, I, like many others, had lost the link to what we most powerfully are and have always been.

INVISIBLE ENERGIES

As difficult as it is to talk about the unseen, most people have a kind of sixth sense about it, a trusting and knowing. We can perceive energy, and have plenty of scientific evidence to know that it exists. Like knowing that the Rocky Mountains exist behind a veil of fog, we have an intuitive sense of the world of energetics, and of the immutable laws that govern how energy operates. We know that when we stub our toe or bang our fingers, we can place a hand over the bruised area and energy begins to transfer, healing us. There are times when we simply "feel" someone enter a room, even if we don't hear or see them; we are responding to their energetic presence.

I (Carole) attended a two-week conference on energy healing some years ago. There I heard a story about a doctor, an oncologist, and how he changed his outlook on trusting what can't be seen.

He told me that at the time of the story, he was having an affair with a woman from his hometown, a small community outside of New York City. This affair had been going on for many years. One day, a patient from his hometown came to see him. The patient needed to have one of his testicles removed, which was cancerous. Since this was the doctor's specialty, he examined the man and agreed to do the surgery.

The operation went well, and in one of the postoperative visits the patient said to the doctor, "I know you are having an affair." He then named the doctor's paramour. The doctor, of course, was flabbergasted. He demanded to know who gave the patient this information.

The patient calmly answered, "Now that I have your attention, I will tell you this. No one told me and I have told no one. I know because I have been undergoing hypnotherapy to help me through the trauma of my operation. And I can tell you this: under anesthesia, everything that goes on in the operating room impacts the patient. I don't care one bit who you are sleeping with but I do care about something else. I hope that you'll stop allowing the attending staff to make comments about the patients. You talked about this affair while you were operating on me. But worse than that, you allowed people to joke about my penis size, and what I would look like with only one testicle!"

The doctor confessed that all of this was true. And he said that this confrontation with his patient changed his life. In that moment he realized that things were not as they appeared on the surface. If his patient could still perceive all of that while his conscious mind was under anesthesia, then the unconscious must have tremendous impact on us, and must also be a source of tremendous potential. The doctor began a journey to learn what it meant to be a healer as well as a doctor. He eventually stopped his affair, told his wife, and entered couples counseling.

It is ridiculous to think that we create life or that we control it, except in some very mundane ways. After all, life got along just fine without us for millions of years. No matter how important we might think we are, and no matter how famous we might become, we are still but a blink of God's eyelid. What if each of us is here simply to contribute something new and unique to the vast pool of life? Then my breath, my struggles, my love, my tears, my voice— perhaps they are enough.

RESTORING BALANCE AND ORDER
THE RAINMAKER

THERE WAS A drought in a village in China. They sent for a rainmaker who was known to live in the farthest corner of the country, far, far away. When the rainmaker arrived, he found the village in a miserable state. Cattle were dying, the vegetation was dying, the people were infected with strange diseases.

The people crowded around the esteemed rainmaker, and were very curious what he would do. He said, "Well, just give me a little hut and leave me alone for a few days."

So the townspeople provided the little hut and he went inside, leaving people to wonder what he would do. One day passed. No rain. A second day passed. Still no rain. On the third day it started pouring, and the rainmaker came out of his hut.

The townspeople applauded his great powers. They asked him, "What did you do? How did you bring the rain?"

"Oh," he said, "Bringing the rain is very simple. I didn't do anything at all."

"But look," they said. "Now it rains. What happened?"

Then the rainmaker said, "I come from an area that is in the Tao, in balance. We have rain, we have sunshine. Nothing is out of order. I come into your area and find that it is chaotic. The rhythm of life is disturbed. When I come into this place, I am disturbed too. The whole thing affects me and I am immediately out of order. So what can I do?

"All I need is a little hut to be by myself, to meditate, to set myself straight. And then, when I am able to get myself in order again, everything around is set right, too. We are now in the Tao, and now it rains; now we are all in the Tao."[7]

Tribal consciousness can bring us into this Tao, can bring balance into our lives. Through the practice of trust and faith, our lives can once again be lived in relationship to the invisible forces that surround us, that shape us.

Trust and faith lead us to service. Service to the tribe gives us the foundation for devotion. Devotion leads us back to trust and faith. It is the practice of knowing and acting from this state of awareness that tells us that we are part of something bigger, that gives us the wisdom to say, "I am not separate from Life."

Tribe sets the stage for connecting to the vaster, unseen flows and forces of life, setting the stage for worship. And worship sets the stage for tribe. We are lost without each, because they are inseparable. They are one.

Voices Of The Tribe

One night a few months ago I was sharing misery with my friend, Chad. His fiancée had dumped him. I was suffering from unrequited love. We were a hurt pair. Chad asked me how I dealt with my pain.

"Meditate."

"I meditate every day. I see it as a commitment to an act of self love, even when my feelings are saying that I am unlovable."

—Wallace Mann

This is how one woman worked with prayer:

> During one of my meditations in Bali, I spontaneously came into a prayer which I repeated each day of my trip there, several times a day:
> "I pray to remember my life and every act of my life as an act of prayer and as an act of grace."
> I struggled to remember this prayer daily, to remember as I walked from my room to the dining area that my walking was an act of prayer and grace. I struggled to remember that as I ate or slept or talked with other members of the group, all of those actions were acts of prayer and grace. And then, somehow, without my noticing, but simply by the intention to live that prayer into existence, I began to see and feel my life as that. I began to feel my every breath as held in a much larger, infinite and vast Life-Intended act of grace, prayer and devotion. I still work with this prayer every day, and it has become like background music, faint and distant, but always playing if I quiet myself enough to hear it.
>
> —Tina Benson

One man's prayer:

> I pray for the strength to open to myself, the enormity of it, the death, the abyss. I understand the courage and the strength and to say yes to my path, my truth, my beauty, my God. Not to deny, resist, push away, but to surrender to an inner "thing." But the fear of that place, the loss of control, the unknown, where nothing is reflected. That ledge where the next step is such a step of total faith as if falling into the hand of God.
>
> —Anonymous

9

THE SEVENTH VALUE:
COMPLETING THE CIRCLE

Your vision will become clear only when you can look
into your own heart... who looks outside dreams, who
looks inside awakes.

—*Carl Jung*

The work of seeing is done
Now practice heart work
Upon those images captive within you.

—*Rainer Maria Rilke*

THIS FINAL TRIBAL value invites us to take each member of
the tribe into our own hearts. It invites us into the realization that everything we see outside of ourselves lives inside us
as well.

Everything that we admire and respect, or fear and judge, in
another has an equivalent inside us. The highest and most sacred function of tribe is to reflect back to us our own inner potential, hidden resource, and vast range. It becomes our sacred responsibility to take the
tribe back inside, to know each member of the tribe as ourselves.

There's a wonderful story which you may have learned in
high school history class that illustrates how this works. The story
goes that when Magellan and his men landed at Tierra del Fuego
they anchored their ships a few hundred yards offshore, then got into
dugout canoes to explore the island and meet the local people.

After many attempts to communicate with the Fuegans,
Magellan and the Fuegan chief were finally able to ask each other a

few simple questions. The chief wanted to know how many moons it had taken for Magellan and his men to get to the island. Magellan responded by telling him it had taken many months of moons. The chief and his men heard this and were in awe, responding as if these men from the sea were gods. Magellan was confused, until he realized that the chief thought they had traveled the entire distance in their canoes!

Wanting to clarify any misconceptions, Magellan pointed to their ships, bobbing in the ocean a few hundred yards from shore. The chief and his people stared out over the waves. "What ships?" they asked, for they could not see them, even though they were clearly visible to all of Magellan's crew. After many failed attempts to point out the ships to the Fuegans, Magellan eventually realized that the Fuegans could not see the ships because there was nothing in prior Fuegan consciousness to prepare them for what they were seeing. Magellan rowed the chief and some of his men out to a ship so they could experience one close up. As the chief and his men stood on the ship and walked around its decks, other villagers on the shore were suddenly able to see it. It was now a reality in the collective consciousness of the Fuegan people![1]

This story brings us to the realization that things may not be as they appear to us; there may be much more to life than we can recognize. If we see or perceive *anything*, it is because its existence is in some way already part of our experience. We just could not see it or perceive it if it weren't already a part of our internal makeup.

This is the most challenging and most rewarding leap that we will make in our move toward tribal consciousness. In the study of human perception—how we learn and how we know—we discover that everything we see in the external world has an inner equivalent. In other words, whatever or whomever we love, respect, wish to emulate, desire—even what we fear and hate—also lives within us in some form. If it didn't, we simply wouldn't notice it. We can know ourselves, and begin to deepen our capacity and our resources, by becoming aware of what we react to in the external world.

It is often difficult for us to accept that this applies equally to those individuals and situations we embrace and to those individuals and situations we reject or abhor. The key, however, is that we have a reaction. Our reaction, either positive or negative, tells us—if we listen—that there's an inner equivalent we can't yet see, but which must have a lot of power within us to produce such a response. If we follow our reaction as our guide, we can find it.

REACTIONS AS OUR GUIDE

I (Carole) remember talking with a friend, Eddie, who had lived in an ashram for several years as the disciple of a famous guru. I was trying to understand how such a well-educated, worldly individual could leave his life and follow this guru from country to country. The words he spoke to me that day moved me deeply. Eddie said he decided this form of worship and devotion would be his path to self-love. He had found it very difficult to love himself, but found it easy to love the guru. In the presence of his guru, he opened to love with a magnitude he had never felt before. In other words, Eddie had a powerful positive projection on his guru. He decided that each day he would sit at the feet of this guru and practice loving him, while at the same time knowing that his love for the guru was really just a projection of his love for himself. Each day Eddie would send his love to the guru, and then imagine that the guru was simply a mirror of himself. He did this for many years.

One day, while sitting in meditation, he finally *knew* that the wisdom, compassion, insight, and love that he felt the guru embraced were actually in himself. He could feel in that moment that the qualities he had imagined belonged to the guru alone also lived inside him. That day, Eddie packed up his few meager possessions and re-entered the world as the wiser man he now knew himself to be. He had access to himself as love.

While many of us would never choose this particular path to our awakening, we may have had the experience of feeling that someone outside ourselves has something we need or want. Sometimes, by choosing to enter into an apprenticeship, be it a highly structured situation (as Eddie experienced when he dedicated himself to his guru), or a more informal one (as when we enter into an intimate personal relationship), we are brought into contact with lost parts of ourselves that are asking to be re-integrated. The person outside us—the guru, the mentor, the lover—usually has qualities we are seeking. If we are having a strong reaction to another person—positive or negative—it means their characteristics also reside within us. One of the most sacred functions of any intimate relationship is that it can bring us into relationship with qualities we most need to recognize in ourselves. Like the guru, our significant others mirror back to us parts of ourselves. One of the sacred practices of relationship is to consciously begin to take those qualities back into ourselves: to know ourselves as *that*.

TAKING IN OUR PROJECTIONS

The popular author Arthur C. Clarke once said, "The person you love does not exist, but is a projection of your innermost desire onto the closest approximate screen." Projection is the process of attributing aspects of ourselves to other people or to situations outside ourselves. While we know that the person we love does indeed exist as an individual separate from us, we also could say that the qualities we experience them as having (particularly the ones we have a strong positive or negative reaction to) are our own qualities as well.

We have a staff member named Bob who vacillates between completely loving and admiring me (Jodi) for my capacity to think things through, problem solve, and organize a large number of tasks concurrently, and thinking I am a horrible, heartless, slave-driving tyrant! While Bob was at a workshop a few months ago, he had a dream in which I was one of the players. Motivated by his dream, he courageously decided to look at what unseen aspects of himself I must symbolically represent for him.

This process of looking in ourselves for the characteristics we attribute to others is called "taking in a projection." Taking in a projection, though the steps are simple, can be emotionally very challenging, since the reason we have a projection in the first place is that the attributes are too hard for us to own directly! Bob had to be both very non-judgmental and very vulnerable. He used some straightforward exercises to help him first identify his projections, and then start to take them in.

As Bob took himself through the following steps, he had revelations that astonished him.

First he decided to look at his negative projections—those things about me to which he reacted negatively. He started to look for his projections through an exercise we call "pointing the finger." He imagined himself standing in front of me, pointing his finger at me, telling me everything he hated about me, with no holds barred. With all of the upset, anger, and judgment he had, he said, "I hate you because you're so_____." "I can't stand you because you_____." He let this process go on for a while, filling in all the blanks, over and over again. He really went for it, holding nothing back. He said all that he had been thinking for the months he had known me.

Bob then got quiet and vulnerable, and asked himself when he had previously felt the same way. He went further back in his life, getting younger in his feelings, allowing any memories, images, or body sensations to surface. Soon he was back in his early childhood with his father, trying so hard, feeling inadequate, and unable to please him no matter what he did.

The last step of this projection process required Bob to look inside himself. Bob saw how he was putting the same pressures on himself that his father had once put on him—regardless of whom he was now working for or where. He slowly became aware of how harsh he was with himself: setting unattainable standards, looking upon himself as inadequate if he needed help, and insisting that anything less than perfection was not okay. He realized that he no longer needed his father to judge him—he was judging himself just as harshly. Bob finally began to accept that his feeling of being judged by others was actually "an inside job."

As Bob worked with himself, and did this same process with his positive projection on me, he began to understand that he had all the wonderful capacities inside him that he imagined I possessed!

This isn't to say that many of the positive and negative things he projected on me aren't accurate (just because we're having a reaction to something outside of us doesn't mean it can't be true, too). But Bob was finally able to take ownership for his part, seeing his projections clearly, and noting that much of what he projected outside himself could be turned around and used as a personal resource, a valuable asset.

Bob began to see that it was possible to tap into his own resources, which were masked behind his projections. He became much more successful at doing his logistics work, much less upset with himself when he made a mistake, and much more able to accept me. Over time, my relationship with Bob has changed to something authentic, because he isn't idolizing me or being upset with me all the time. We are able to meet as equals, learning from each other and enjoying each other's presence.

Now, you might wonder why we are discussing this in a book about tribe. The answer is simple. Just as our intimate relationships mirror back aspects of ourselves, so the tribe mirrors back to us a larger internal reality. When we come out of isolation and experience others participating in our lives and endeavors, we feel relief that we are not alone, that we don't have to be all things to all people. Imagine making the next leap, which is the living realization that all the richness, wisdom, capacity, and personality that holds you within its tribal arms, is indeed a reflection of your own inner world!

INNER RESOURCE FROM OUTER TRIBE

When Zachary was born, I (Carole) had never spent much time around children. He was my first experience of having to be responsible as a mother. Moreover, my own mother had been sick and institutionalized during much of my childhood, so I hadn't had much mothering when I was a child myself. I then had two ways to begin learning how to mother. One way was to simply open my heart to Zachary and begin responding to his needs. The other way was to be in tribe with other parents, to sit with women who were mothers, and simply be with them as they mothered their children.

Often, the more seasoned moms would intervene with Zach in a helpful way. I might have let all my development as a mother stop right there. I could have simply made a point to be around a lot of other women, thus guaranteeing that Zach would get all the mothering he needed. But to do that, I would have had to live within that tribe forever, which I couldn't do. What I could do, though, was take the templates of mothering that Zach and I were witnessing back inside me. I longed to find a capable mother inside of me. As I sat with other mothers, I would ask myself, "Is there anyone inside me who can be like that?" Lo and behold, I began to have dreams that showed me my own inner mother. I somehow began to spontaneously *know* how to reach out to Zachary in ways that previously seemed beyond my grasp. I was beginning to find my inner equivalent of the outer tribe of mothers!

COMPLETING THE CIRCLE

As we enter a new millennium, we find ourselves living in a shrinking world with disintegrating boundaries. Between advances in computer technology and increasingly accessible travel, there are probably few if any tribes left on earth that have not been touched in some way by the world outside their own tribal reality. It's unlikely we'll return to living in a small tribal order, hidden away somewhere in the wilderness, untouched by the world at large. Such a return is not what we advocate here.

For us to live in tribe today, we must let go of the ideal that we can or would even want to exactly recreate Hmong tribal life in our lives. Most of us either couldn't or wouldn't choose to live collectively. The idea is not to preserve an outmoded ideal of tribe—even the Hmong are dying out, their villages inundated with tourists, their children leaving to seek a modern education and the rewards of entrepreneurial life. The idea is to bring alive a new one.

The new tribalism asks us to let go of the notion that the tribe is something that exists only outside of us. This new tribalism invites us to complete the circle by taking the whole tribe back inside each of us, by finding an inner equivalent of our external tribe.

To make this work, we need to relate to the people in our lives—our friends, lovers, co-workers, children—as if they're a symbolic reflection of our own internal cast of characters.

For example, as we glance across the dinner table at our children, we may think, "Do I still have a curious, open-hearted child somewhere inside of me, too?"

At a business meeting or a tough negotiation, we'd look at an executive we admire and ask, "I wonder how I can find a part of myself that's just as strong a leader?"

At a party or social event where we're feeling slightly awkward, we'd see someone completely enjoying themselves and say to ourselves, "There must be someone inside of me who can be just as confident and spontaneous."

Remember, the only reason we'd notice any of their characteristics is if we already had an inner equivalent. If we're willing to take in our tribe, we can welcome the people in our lives not just like they're others, separate from us, but like they're parts of ourselves.

With this simple change in perception, each tribe member becomes a gift to us, each one holding perspectives and capacities that we, too, can learn to embody. Even the idea that this *might* be true allows for a level of sharing, compassion, and richness not available from our separation. This change guides us to a new range of ability within ourselves, freeing us from living in the narrow confines of our usual perception. It also leads us to view others with a heightened respect and appreciation. The following is a beautiful story that was told to us by a participant in one of our workshops:

THE RABBI'S GIFT

LONG AGO, there was an ancient monastery which had fallen into disrepair, since interest in the monastic life had waned in recent years. There were only five monks left, the abbot himself and four priests, all over seventy years of age.

In the woods near the monastery was a little hut that from time to time was used by a rabbi for prayer and study. The monks could always tell when the rabbi was in the hut, and one day the abbot decided to go and visit the rabbi, to ask his counsel about what to do to revive his dying order.

The abbot went to the hut, knocked on the door, and was warmly welcomed by the rabbi. When he related his dilemma, the rabbi could only commiserate, saying, "I know what you mean. Everywhere, people have forgotten about the old ways, and they turn away from God. The light and the spirit have gone out of the people."

And so the old priest and the rabbi sat together, praying, talking, weeping for what had been lost. When it was time for the abbot to leave, the rabbi said to him, "I am sorry that I could not give you more help or advice. All I can tell you is that the Messiah is one of you."

When the abbot returned to the monastery, the anxious monks were waiting for him at the door. "What did the rabbi say?" they asked.

"Well," replied the abbot, "it was wonderful sitting with him. We talked and prayed and read. But he couldn't really help. The only thing he did say was that the Messiah is one of us. I am not even sure what he meant by that."

In the days and weeks that followed, the old monks pondered the rabbi's words. The Messiah is one of us? Did he mean here at the monastery? Surely he couldn't have meant that literally. But if he did, to whom could he have been referring? Could he have meant the abbot? Yes, if he meant any of us, surely it was the abbot. He has been our leader for more than a generation. On the other hand, could he have meant Brother Thomas? Certainly Thomas is a holy man. He mustn't have meant Brother Eldred. He gets so crotchety at times, but come to think of it, even though he is a thorn in people's sides, he is usually right! Maybe he did mean Brother Eldred! Surely not Brother Philip. He is so passive, hardly ever speaks. But he does seem to have a gift for being there just when you need him, in a silent, supportive way. Maybe Philip is the Messiah. Of course he couldn't mean me. I am just an ordinary person, nothing special. But suppose that he did mean me? Oh, God, not me!

On and on it went. As each of the old monks contemplated the riddle in this manner, they began to treat each other with extraordinary respect, on the off chance that one of them might be the Messiah. And, just in case they themselves might be the Messiah, they began to treat themselves with the most extraordinary respect, too.

The monastery was situated in a beautiful forest, and every so often people would come there to picnic on its grounds, which were still inviting. As they did so, without even being conscious of it, they could feel the aura of love and respect that permeated the entire place. It was so compelling, they began to come more often, and they would bring their friends to picnic, play, and pray in this special place. Then, some of the young men started to talk with the old monks. After a while, one man asked if he could join them, and then another, and another. So it came to pass that within a few years the monastery became a thriving order once again.

What had changed to make the monastery thrive? Each monk had found the qualities and attributes of the Messiah in his outer tribe, as well as in himself. Once this simple shift of perception had begun, the tribe began to flourish.

WHERE DO WE GO TO BELONG?

Our society is a lot like the monks' world in the story. Just as the monks' monastery was falling into disrepair, so too are parts of our social structure. Government-run healthcare programs are being dismantled. No matter how large or profitable the corporation, our idea of job security is becoming just a memory. No longer can we be certain that if we just work hard enough and pay our taxes, we'll be carried cradle to grave. But in the same way the monks started to treat each other with more respect, we're making some small cultural changes too. Some businesses have started on-site day care programs for the children of their employees, while other companies are allowing employees to spend more time working from home. Farmers are starting to talk more seriously about sustainable agriculture.

We're starting to see our cultural pendulum swing from structures based solely on patriarchal values back towards ones which include balancing feminine values, such as creating, nurturing, and sustaining. The pendulum hasn't swung very far, but it has changed direction.

So when the systems that have defined our social roles and relationships for us start to change, and our predictable place in our families and our communities no longer exists, what do we do? Where do we go to belong?

We can to go to our own inner tribe to belong.

We believe that a new tribal order can lead us to recognition, maturation, and the development of ourselves. In contemporary culture, tribes are moving and fluid gatherings, not lockstep organizations of followers. As we use these diverse gatherings to reflect back to ourselves who we are, we mature, deepen, and flower. And as we start to recognize ourselves, we start to recognize ourselves in each other.

In every workshop we ask, "How many of you know that you are a multiplicity of selves, not just one?" Many hands go up, and then the discussion begins. We learn that each of us has experienced that we are not the same person when we are working as when we are making love, parenting our children, or visiting a friend in need. We have a whole internal world of selves. If we look upon ourselves only as our outer personality, the small part that we feel safe presenting to the world, we miss the whole inner spectrum.

Each one of us embodies archetypal patterns: Shaman, Sage, Hero, Lover, Warrior, Trickster, Parent, Wise Woman, Wounded Child, and many others. To connect to with these parts of ourselves, we must practice our tribal values with our internal tribe. Ultimately this means parenting, mentoring, and recognizing ourselves. It means exploring the qualities and capacities that we see in others in ourselves. We would express ourselves in new ways, and risk participating in situations that challenge and stretch us.

Embracing this new vision of our lives gives us access to much vaster resources than we have ever had before. When we begin a relationship with the internal equivalent of members of our tribal circle—grandfather and grandmother, medicine man or high priest, warrior, lover—they're always with us, available for us to access on our own.

We can find our inner tribe not only through outer reflection. They also show themselves all the time as characters in our dreams, symbols and texture in our art, and forms in our dance.

THE INNER LANDSCAPE

So often we reject parts of ourselves. How many times have you thought, "If only I weren't so..." You fill in the blanks: scared, destructive, wimpy, overbearing, or a thousand other criticisms. Any time we try to eradicate something in ourselves, it only seems to get stronger, more dominant. Yet, by observing those same qualities reflected in tribe members around us, we can sometimes see how those same qualities can serve.

Oddly enough, the parts of ourselves that we reject become unconscious motivation; hiding and denying what we can't accept in ourselves. For example, the person who says, "I won't become like my father," soon falls into behavior patterns skewed towards avoidance of their father's traits. But you can see that this person is still being motivated by their father's behaviors!

It's only when we stop rejecting parts of ourselves that we have some chance at wholeness. In our example, we would have to start opening to whatever ways we may be just like our father. Of course, given our strong reaction to those parts, this might be difficult! Our response would probably be to insist, "No! I'm not like him." But if we can start to open, without self-judgment, to even the possibility that we may have some aspects that are like our father, then ever so slowly we can start to see, get to know, and accept those parts of ourselves. And then instead of battling with our internal forces, we can start to consciously participate with them.

It's absolutely critical to realize that just because we can identify some of those same attributes within ourselves, does not mean we have to use them the same way that our father did. The point of trying to reintegrate them is to learn to *not* use them the same way, which we can do only through consciously accepting them.

If this talk about the denying and rejecting of unconscious motivation seems to hard to accept, well, that's a perfectly natural reaction!

To keep going with our example, let's say our father was very bossy, very controlling. We all know how unpleasant it can be to be around someone like this. Yet we can see how being able to control, how to be the one in charge, is also the essence of being a strong leader. If we simply reject being controlling, then we also reject any possibility of leadership. The problem isn't with the force of control, it's with how our father used it.

Or let's say our father was very dependent, very needy. We may have decided for ourselves we would never be that dependent on anyone. But if we do this, then we also lose the ability to ask for help, and we live our lives isolated. Again, the force of need isn't good or bad by itself, it's whether we can use it consciously—or whether it unconsciously drives us.

Whatever we see, admire, and recognize in another is in us. Instead of trying so hard to change and control things and people in the outer world with which we're at odds, we can begin finding an equivalent within ourselves. It is here with our inner tribe that we can truly heal, and make peace with the rejected parts of ourselves. It's so much easier to accept ourselves than to change the entire world!

When we pull our projections from the world and take ownership of them, our world becomes safer and more available. Then the next time an upsetting image turns up in our outer world we're able to transform its impact on us, and handle it constructively and creatively. We now begin to have choices about how we relate to the world when those difficult situations arise. Things can be what they are, and we can relate to them with resource.

INNER AND OUTER IN BALANCE

In Kenya several years ago, I (Jodi) went on safari at Masai Mara National Park. We were on an early morning game drive on the Serengeti plains, and saw some activity in the distance. As we got closer, within about 15 feet of the animals, we saw two lions devouring a gazelle. They were tearing it apart, growling as they did, their faces smeared with blood. My first response was to look away—feeling frightened and sad for the gazelle. My friend Liza encouraged me to take a deep breath, and look again. This time I felt the rumbling in my own belly, and with it the magnificence of the power and the strength of the lion and its ability to feed itself and its cubs, and the beauty of the gazelle's death sacrificed to give life to the lion. The lions ate until they fell into satiated slumber, and everything was as it should be that morning.

We don't blame the lion for killing and eating a gazelle. In the grand scheme of things, that is part of life's balance. The lion takes what it needs, naturally keeping the balance for the gazelles as well as itself. It takes some effort for those of us who have been protected from such sights to be able to view them as expressions of order and harmony. As human beings, it is important for us to accept the world and all its forces, the ones we like and the ones we don't, back into our hearts.

When we know that nothing exists outside of God, and can honor our own inner temple of wholeness, our lives come into balance. The inner and the outer become synergistic, not only balancing one another but building on each other's creative powers.

Knowing all of life's forces reside within, feeling ourselves as the earth, the planets, as another who is suffering or struggling, is imperative. If we don't know the equivalent of the whole tribe inside, then our actions occur out of relationship to the totality, to God. I can only wound the earth if I think I am somehow separate from it. I can only ignore a person's suffering if I haven't yet found the same kind of suffering within myself.

Of course, reclaiming ourselves requires we be willing to feel so many of those feelings we've wanted to avoid. China Galland, author of *Longing for Darkness*, poignantly describes our dilemma:

"Our choice is to be in love or in fear. But to choose to be in love means to have a mountain inside of you, means to have the heart of the world inside of you, means you will feel another's suffering inside your own body and you will weep. You will have no protection from the world's pain because it will be your own."[2]

No wonder we sometimes want to believe ourselves separate from the rest of our world.

Anything that has power over us we will reject, including anything that resides within us. My salvation lies in knowing that it, he, she, the forces, all of them—all and everything!—are in me. Slowly I begin to have an inner relationship to them. Slowly I build a temple of love and compassion in which all of life's forces are held and enacted in wholeness and balance.

SYMBOLS OF OUR SOULS

Some years ago, I (Jodi) was part of a Jungian study group with a wonderful teacher named Edith Sullwold. On the first weekend we gathered, we spent a great deal of time meditating, painting, working with clay, and listening to poetry. By Sunday morning, I could feel my anxiety rising as the group began to wind down. I wondered if what I did over the weekend had any value, and how I would use it in my life. I impatiently raised my hand and asked Edith a series of questions. In her quiet wisdom she gently said to me, "Jodi, there is so much you don't know about yourself—you are as vast as the ocean, and don't even know it. One would hope that you would take your art work home, and look at it for five minutes every morning when you wake, and let the mystery of who you are, which you have expressed in this artwork, speak to you each day. Then you can return to us next month, and educate us about the value of using your imagination."

There is an unconscious process living in and through each

of us. One of the sacred functions of tribe is to reflect it back to us. As we begin to directly connect to and share the inner symbols and images that come from the unconscious, we renew and enrich not only ourselves, but our entire tribe. The following example illustrates this beautifully.

Barbara had spent her lifetime hating her body. She was a tall, large-boned woman, whose mother had told her over and over again to diet, to take dance lessons, anything to become more like her petite younger sister. One day, in a tribal gathering, Barbara came in from doing some soul work. She had been moved to work in clay, after one session where the women spoke about the grief they felt in not being able to love their bodies. They had spoken of their self-hatred, their trying to manage that hatred through diet, their attempts at physical perfection.

Barbara brought in her sculptures, which she had been working on for several days. As she showed the progression of work, every man and woman in the circle was moved to tears. She told of how, on the first day, all she could do was sit in front of a lump of clay and weep, unable to touch it, unsure even of how it should look. So, for the first day, she sat with her grief.

On the next day, she was able to place her hands on the clay, and she began to form a body. She could feel that this was the body of a young girl, undeveloped, a beginning. What Barbara noticed most was that she felt protective of this young girl, could feel her uncertainty, and her desire to stretch out with her young limbs and feel the world. As Barbara began forming the clay with her hands, she could feel it inside her own body.

As the days went by, clay images began to take shape. Each day as she sat with the clay she could feel the feelings that had been repressed for so long, her sensuality, her love of her body, her shame, her withdrawal, until she showed us the final sculpture of a full-hipped, full-bodied woman.

Barbara said, "As I formed her I could feel such love for her, and I knew that she was me. It was no longer a concept that I should love myself, but as I placed my hands upon her to form her, I loved her shape so much! I knew that she was a woman, that she was rich and sensual, expressive, warm, vital. I felt as though I was beginning to know and love myself."

As Barbara shared her journey with the group, each member of the group could begin to accept similar aspects of themselves. The same thing happens every time we gather as a tribe and simply share our nighttime dreams. We don't need to know what they mean, we don't have to interpret each other's art or poetry, or dreams, or dance, we simply need to witness it, to be in the presence of it, to be enriched and moved.

We have all been inspired when someone shares from their heart, when they take the risk to tell us what moves them, to express what they love, envision, and care about. It doesn't mean we must take on the same values as they do. But imagine if, within the tribe, such vulnerable, tender sharing was always available. Not only would we keep the link to the richness of soul and spirit, but we would be in the presence of our own reflection, the reflection of our beauty, our magnificence, the forces that we desperately need inside.

THE GREAT WHEEL

Human tribe is but one piece of the great wheel of life. Tribes have gathered throughout time to honor and witness the animals, the elements, the ancestors, the vast forces that can't be seen. Each of us issues through a lineage, with its own history, stories, traditions, and practices, extending back through time, to foreign lands, ancient ancestors, beyond what is available to us through our everyday memories. We can not only take back in the people who are currently in our lives, we can also reclaim and reintegrate the tribe of our ancestors. The memories of our ancestors exist in us on a cellular level, and our dreams often bring us the images that call us back home to our ancient tribal clan. The following piece was written after a two week conference of ours, called Pathways, by an American woman of Samoan lineage:

THE NECKLACE

WAKING UP FROM deep sleep, the dream was still vivid. I was walking alongside a beautiful seashore with my mother, my heart filled with love and joy. After some time, we stopped walking and my mother silently reached over to put a delicate necklace made of animal teeth and wood around my neck. I felt honored but unsure of my mother's intention. The dream ended. It wasn't until the last day of silence and fasting during the workshop (which coincidentally was my mother's birthday), that I felt in my body and my soul, the symbolic and sacred meaning of the necklace. As the sun set that day, I performed an ancient ritual ceremony with two of my Pathways sisters, intuitively letting the rhythm of the wind and the spirits of my ancestors guide me. By using intention and calling in the forces, the three of us managed to re-create the "Kava Ceremony," a dance my mother performed for honored chiefs in her village, fulfilling her duty as the chief's daughter. Later in the workshop, I danced the Kava Ceremony for the whole workshop group, and felt so witnessed and honored by the assembled tribe, my current tribe. Two years later, I continue to work with the images of that dream and have learned that the necklace represents the generational "passing of the mantle." Perhaps life asks that I serve as a bridge, connecting my Samoan ancestors to my future lineage.

In all days and ages there were mystery schools, schools for the study of the invisible. Tribe was connected to and in service to the invisible realms, and man was in service to the tribe. How do we get there from here in our modern world? How do we reconnect to the mystery of life when our tribe has lost its rites and rituals, even when we have lost tribe itself? There are two gates: the tribe can slowly reinstate the rites that connect it to life's unseen forces, and as individuals, we can begin to have the courage to claim the inner tribe and internally connect to our symbols and imaginations, dreams, and fantasies. As we do so, we begin to restore our balance, remember our humanity, and renew our world.

Voices Of The Tribe

This was written by a man after a guided meditation in a tribal gathering:

As I was watching this scene, it came to me that I could do this in my own soul by bringing together my feminine aspect, my aware adult self, and the little boy I still carried within me. We were a family, in the same sacred circle of my own heart. I felt the deep water of a great truth stir inside me as a rush of goose-bumps rippled across my skin. I had never felt so complete. And though an unbelievable sense of relief flooded over me, I did not cry. I felt solid, expectant.

After all the longing and loneliness, it seemed like such a simple discovery. I had found within me the companionship I had ached for, and no matter where I went or who passed through—or stayed—in my life, I would never be alone again. I had come home.[3]

—Paul Seaman

Here is a woman's poem written about a piece of soul work she had created:

As I sculpt the woman
Sitting on the rock
At times I feel I am touching myself

At times I am touching my mother
At times I am touching my lover

They all blend into one
One woman
Who I have seen and known

She was calling,
The clay was calling
She is thick around the hips
Just like me
Arms funny, just like me
Full thighs, just like me.

—Jan Cohn

This is a woman's body dialoguing with her:

So, tell me arms, what are you reaching for?
I'm saying, "YES."
Yes to what?
Yes to you.
What do you mean?
You have spent a lifetime saying no to your own honest and free
self-expression. You have not given me freedom.
What do you want?
I want you to surrender yourself—to show yourself honestly, to
reveal yourself nakedly and without pretense. I want you to feel the freedom
of your own body as it moves—to feel your arms as they paint without
judgment or direction. I want you to choose yes.
To reveal yourself nakedly and honestly.

Why now?
Because you know enough now to trust me.
　　　　　　　　　　　—Tina Benson

This is a reflection about the partnership of man and God:

Lenses and light are fundamentally different from one another. Light is a wave of energy, flowing continuously; the lens is matter, static and fixed. Yet these two opposites are partners, each needing the other. As the stream of light interacts with the lens, the light becomes directed... and together they take on a new purpose, to illuminate something which is neither the light nor the lens.

Just as the light and the lens create together, the consciousness that I am must be formed through such a partnership. There is an energy flowing through me, a magic that is not just my flesh and blood. What is this energy that animates me? How do I honor my unspoken partnership with it? And what do we work together to reveal?

The lens that focuses the light is not the light. And the light is not that which it illuminates.
　　　　　　　　　　　—Bruce McDiffett

PART

III

PRACTICING THE VALUES

IN MODERN LIFE

Many of us are acquainted with the wonderful teaching story about an adolescent boy who goes to live in the Zendo, intent on studying with a great Buddhist Master. After a few days anxiously awaiting his first interview, the boy is finally summoned to the Master's quarters and a teacup is placed before him.

As the tea is brewing, the boy begins telling the Master how eager he is to learn. He tells him about everything he has done to prepare himself for his work at the Zendo. He lists the books he has read and says how many hours each day he meditates. He recounts his discussions with other students and teachers.

With a steady gaze the Master listens to the boy, nods, and smiles. When the boy has finished what he has to say, the Master picks up the teapot and pours and pours and pours until the tea is running over the cup and saucer, onto the table and to the floor. The boy is alarmed and confused, not knowing how to respond to the Master's actions.

With the contents of the teapot exhausted, the Master looks at the boy and says, "Until you have emptied yourself of all that you think you know, I can teach you nothing." And with that, he walks out of the room.

Imagine the luxury of *not knowing*. Like the boy in this story, most of us are taught that not knowing is a weakness. We might be ashamed, embarrassed, or even threatened to imagine being discovered in our ignorance. We take great pride in our knowledge, wearing it like a badge of honor. While none would argue that knowledge enriches our lives, the pride associated with knowing can also impair our ability to grow and change.

Consider how thoroughbreds are trained. The trainer is taking the finest quality of horse and, through a constant series of challenges, refining the way it walks, runs, and jumps. But the training starts with the awareness that this horse already has the raw talent, breeding, and capacity to be a world-class competitor. The trainer's job is to develop that horse to the highest degree of excellence. We invite you to approach this section of the book in that same spirit, that you are already a world-class thoroughbred. Approach this work with what the Buddhists call a "beginner's mind," that is, from a perspective of *not knowing*.

As you begin to develop tribal consciousness, your actions and some of your greatest contributions will come from knowledge and skills that you already have. Over time, other like-minded individuals will join your tribe, bringing their creative energies to the tribe as well.

It isn't enough to just want tribe; there are specific actions required for creating it. While we might observe some already-functioning tribe from a distance and conclude that these actions flow automatically and spontaneously, the truth is that they are an explicit part of that tribe's culture. Members draw from a rich reserve of tribal knowledge, supported by daily rituals that we, as outside observers, might not even notice. To create your own tribal dynamics, you are going to need some guidelines and practices that you can bring into your lives.

The basic practices outlined in the following chapter will one day seem automatic. Until then, since we don't live in a modern version of the Hmong village, the guidelines we describe can provide some structure. They help us know what to do about our tribal longing by showing us where to begin, and by giving us a road map for successful tribal living.

So where do we begin? The movement from me and mine to us and ours is simple, but involves skills and awareness that must be practiced. It requires mindfulness, devotion, and tenacity. We have found that the results of these practices are immediate, fulfilling, and well worth it.

Begin these practices wherever you are in your life. Start with one other person, with your family and loved ones, with your colleagues at work, within a larger community, or simply with yourself.

Tribe exists everywhere people gather: in parks, at home, or at the office. You can start in any of these places. You might want to reach out to your friends, or your neighborhood, gathering a few like-minded people who are also looking for a deeper sense of community. Our communities began simply. They began with friends reaching out to friends, inviting them into simple rituals and councils. What began small, grew and grew to include thousands of families, friends, and work groups, all celebrating tribe!

This section is divided into two parts. The first part describes "The Ten Core Tribal Practices." Each of them can work anywhere you have a common desire to knit lives together with more meaning and purpose, with more shared values. Through the years, we and our participants have used these basic exercises in families and intimate relationships, in communities and corporations, and even in each of our relationships with ourselves.

In the second part, "Getting Started," we offer you a set of simple suggestions for implementing these Core Tribal Practices in a variety of settings. Use these ways to begin, and feel free to let your imagination flow with ideas about how you can begin to create tribe in your communities. You'll probably be relieved to learn that getting this to work doesn't take every single person in the tribe practicing all of these things at the same time. When you try even small new things people will begin to respond differently to you. Over and over again we have seen that even one person can make a difference—so empty your teacup and get started!

10

THE TEN CORE TRIBAL PRACTICES

CORE TRIBAL PRACTICE ONE
STAND IF YOU...

INTRODUCTION

Every tribe needs to know its members and what life experiences they bring to the circle. What does each member have to teach, mentor and contribute to the tribe? *Stand If You...* is a powerful way for each member to be recognized for their life experiences. It's a highly effective ritual, easy to do, and most people will feel comfortable doing it.

You'll find that *Stand If You...* brings a new group together quickly, and deepens the resources of an existing tribe. While excellent as a way to initiate the tribe, we find that as a recurring ritual it renews tribal bonds and relationships as members' lives move forward and change.

PREPARATION

Have at least a few pre-determined categories for the tribe to work with. These can be as simple as, "Stand if you are married," or, "Stand if you are divorced," or, "Stand if you own a business." Once you begin, you'll find that one category will suggest another, and there will be a steady flow of questions that arise either from you or from others in the circle.

PROCESS

Once the preparations are completed, the exercise progresses through the following four steps.

STEP 1: THE CIRCLE FORMS. Tribe members are seated in a circle, leaving open space in the center of the room. One person is appointed as the leader.

STEP 2: STAND IF YOU... The exercise begins with the leader saying, "Stand if you...," followed by one of the categories noted on the list. For example, "Stand if you are considering a change in your career or profession." Then, all members who have had that life experience stand up. It's up to each individual to decide what they stand for at any time.

STEP 3: CHECKING IN. Those standing might want to notice how it feels to be standing in this way, witnessed by others in their tribe for that particular life passage. The group that is seated may wish to consider the wisdom gained by those who are standing, and what it feels like to be on the other side of that same experience.

For example, perhaps there are several people standing because they are out of work as a result of downsizing at their place of employment. Maybe you were in that position six months ago, though you are employed now, and at the time you felt very alone. Now, seeing so many people standing for that same reason, your perspective about that life event might shift, and you may be able to look back at that time when you were unemployed with new eyes. You might even find yourself wanting to step in and offer yourself as a mentor to help these fellow tribe members through what you know can be a difficult passage.

STEP 4: NEXT CATEGORY. After a few moments, those who are standing take their seats again and the next category is called out. Proceed through the prepared categories, then open to any questions from the group.

CLOSURE
You might want to leave time at the end of the exercise to give people an opportunity to seek out anyone they wish to talk with. They

may want to ask more questions, or share more deeply their thoughts and feelings about a particular life experience.

You might specifically instruct people to look around the room and connect with a person who has gone through something they are just now entering. For example, a woman pregnant with her first child might want to connect with a woman who has three grown children. A man who is thinking about starting his own business might want to talk with a woman who already has a successful business going. Or a person who once had a particular illness and has now recovered might offer to mentor a person who has just learned that she has that illness.

Additionally, with an ongoing group, you might want to encourage people to begin looking to each other for possible mentor relationships. Reflect openly and enthusiastically about the resources available in this room.

CORE TRIBAL PRACTICE TWO
STORYTELLING

INTRODUCTION

Everyone has a story to tell, and people love to both tell and listen! It was through telling stories that the earliest tribes passed along their collective wisdom, and enjoyed their time together. For example, to hear a fellow tribe member's story about attending the birth of her grandchild fills all the listeners with a sense of awe. The story itself becomes a celebration of the mystery of life that we all share.

Every life experience has a story behind it. In the process of telling our stories to others, we receive affirmation for those experiences. In addition, when we have shared our stories, we discover once again what lessons we have gained through living, while our listeners gain the benefit of them as well. You'll find you only need to focus on a topic and the stories will burst forth, with richness and vitality! Keep the topics focused on life experiences. We learn most of what we know about life by watching how others handle their lives, and hearing them tell stories and anecdotes about experiences they've had.

PREPARATION
Set a time for storytelling to take place. Pick some sample topics to start people off, such as "Your most inspiring accomplishment," or "A time you faced and conquered a fear."

Place a time limit on each story; we suggest approximately six to ten minutes. Stories are best told unrehearsed, so prep time on the story is not recommended. It is also useful to decide in advance how many stories will be told in that session.

PROCESS
STEP 1. Tribe members sit in a circle. Storytelling circles work best with groups of ten or less, allowing time for as many members who wish to offer their stories to do so. Make sure people aren't asked to listen to more stories than they can stay present and alert for.

STEP 2. Introduce the session by assuring people that the point here is to tell a story drawn from their own life experience, speaking casually, as they might relate to a close friend. You're not looking for a "performance," but for real-life experiences told candidly.

STEP 3. Encourage people to listen without commenting or interrupting, and to thank the storytellers as they finish.

STEP 4. Let the group know that each story doesn't have to go the full time. If anyone wants to tell more than one story, it's best to wait until everyone who wants to tell a story has had a chance to do so.

CLOSURE
After all the stories have been told, you might want to take a few minutes to have people talk about what it was like to tell their stories and hear others tell theirs. Did telling or hearing the stories offer you any new perspectives?

CORE TRIBAL PRACTICE THREE
COUNCILS

INTRODUCTION

Often when we get together to take on a problem or difficult issue, we are pretty much oriented toward seeking a resolution, that is, to "problem solve." By contrast, the tradition of the council is to simply give voice to an issue. Positions are not argued; they are only heard. There is an inherent wisdom in this process, because it can be useful to express ourselves, listen to others, and then go away to digest what we've experienced. Many indigenous peoples called this process the *Council Wheel*.

Holding council is very powerful. It honors a basic truth, that most problems and difficult issues arise because we do not even know the right questions to ask. Standing on our own, we can only see through the narrow window of our own perspective. Council can broaden that perspective immensely. Instead of solutions being imposed, a synergy is created that often dissolves the problem discussed.

Sometimes councils are stepping stones, leading to action at a later time. One enters and leaves these councils not with the idea of making a decision but of collecting information, opinions, feelings and experiences that are held by the tribe. In a very real way, councils display what is felt by the tribe, without making judgments, drawing conclusions, or imposing change.

PREPARATION

Choose a place and time where you can hold council with the fewest possible distractions. You will be meeting in a circle configuration, so that everyone has an equal position at the wheel. Your purpose is to create a sacred space, where the dynamics of the council take precedence over everything else. People taking part should be cautioned that they cannot come and go to take care of other business, and that coming in late or leaving early is discouraged. Note that the respect garnered here has to do with respecting the tribe itself as an entity to be honored and nurtured.

Virtually any topic can be suggested for council meetings. But when there is a highly controversial topic, you might need a council facilitator. The council facilitator's role can be challenging. As a facilitator, you might have to make certain that the rules of the "talking stick" are honored: that one person does not interrupt another, belittle them, or attack their positions. Council is a time to present your viewpoint, not as an absolute truth, but as an expression that needs to be heard in a respectful way.

The "talking stick" is a piece of ritual paraphernalia that helps to define the council setting. The stick can be anything easily held in one's hand. Some tribes like to have a stick that has been decorated, or in some way symbolizes the tribe. For example, one group had a rosewood branch with short twigs growing out in many directions. The group chose it because of its natural form, with numerous twigs, suggesting the many different experiences and viewpoints tribe members had to offer each other.

PROCESS

STEP 1. In the first council, the facilitator introduces the talking stick. He or she holds it in their hand as they speak, explaining that anyone who wishes to speak can do so only if they hold the stick.

The talking stick is originally placed in the center of the circle. When a person wishes to speak, they must retrieve it from that place. Holding the talking stick signals all the others that it is this person's turn to speak and for the others to listen.

STEP 2. Whoever picks up the stick can speak as long as they want—without interruption, questions, comments, or responses from the group.

STEP 3. When any person is done speaking, they replace the talking stick in the center of the circle. The next person to take the stick then talks, and when they are finished, returns the stick to the center.

Not everyone is required to speak; a person may also speak as often as he or she likes. Often during a council there can be periods of silence, and this can be quite valuable.

STEP 4. In the beginning, some people might find this way of meeting too formal, too "unnatural," or unproductive because it allows no room for argument, rebuttal, or decision making. But as people express themselves in council, they will begin to discover its magic. Amazingly, the synergy of the tribe takes over and issues not only find solutions, but seem to almost work themselves out. The tribe becomes stronger and stronger, learning about the powerful resources they hold in their number.

CLOSURE

It's best to have a time limit for holding council, thus ending by the clock. One person should be in charge of the clock, giving a five-minute warning before bringing the council to a close. The person closing the circle should thank all who are present for taking part in this council, with a reminder that by taking part in this process they help to build the power and integrity of the tribe.

In the first few councils, the last person who takes up the talking stick may wish to instruct those who have taken part in this council to hold the council sacred. The opinions, insights, and self-disclosures which are made possible through council need to be honored, respected and held in confidence by all.

CORE TRIBAL PRACTICE FOUR
OFFERING RECOGNITION

INTRODUCTION

It's very effective to meet with work groups, families, spouses, friends, or any group you are involved with in an ongoing way, to develop ways to give and receive recognition. The practice of recognition provides the structure for personal validation, reflection and encouragement. This process is simple, well worth the investment of time, and personally satisfying for all who participate.

As we integrate the practice of recognition into our lives, each member of the tribe becomes increasingly aware of what they have to offer. In this way, we don't have to resort to huge, heroic accomplishments in order to get much-needed acknowledgment, and our everyday actions become seen and appreciated in a new light. Within any tribal organization, giving and receiving recognition builds the strength of each individual and thus the strength of the whole.

PREPARATION

Your ultimate goal in this process is to develop an awareness of the power of recognition, and to encourage giving and receiving it as an everyday habit. Preparation should include having at least one meeting in which you discuss the importance of recognition, how to express it to others in a way that is sincere and meaningful, how to receive it, and how to ask for it. The steps described below should be reviewed as part of your preparation.

PROCESS

STEP 1. Recognition works best when it describes a specific behavior, when the statement of recognition is brief, and when the recognition is expressed as an "I" statement. Here are some examples that we have found work well:

> I saw you take a risk by _____.
> I noticed that you _____.
> I appreciate you when you _____.
> I am aware of the efforts you are making to _____.
> You were courageous when you _____.
> I am learning from you as you _____.
> _____ made a difference for me today.

STEP 2. When you receive recognition, respond with as few words as possible. A simple "thank you" is sufficient. No need to explain why you did what you did, or to offer recognition in return.

Be particularly careful about deflecting the recognition you receive, or debating about the content. The usual ways we do this are with statements such as, "It wasn't that big a deal," or "I was only doing my job," or, "Well, Joe was really the one who should get the credit."

When you are receiving recognition, listen. Let your mind be still and your heart be open. Take in how you are being witnessed at that moment. Acknowledge the person who takes time to recognize you by thanking them and taking pleasure in what they are giving you.

STEP 3. In your daily life, look for opportunities to give recognition, whether you do it on an informal, one-to-one basis, or in a meeting where you announce that you would like to recognize a certain person.

CLOSURE
When giving recognition, do so with no strings attached. Keep in mind that the goal is not to flatter but to acknowledge a person for something they have done. Their gratitude completes the recognition and brings the process to a close.

CORE TRIBAL PRACTICE FIVE
RITUAL

INTRODUCTION
Ritual is a powerful tool for entering tribal consciousness and creating change. Rituals mark and celebrate life passages, and alert the whole tribe to new developments. Rituals can also be simple, helping to link us to the sacred in our daily lives. These might include rituals for coming home at the end of the day, rituals for creating intimacy, rituals at meal or bedtimes, rituals to welcome the seasons, for the full moon, the solstices, birthdays, and special holidays. You probably already have rituals in many areas of your life, both personal ones and ones that you do with others. Regardless of your intention for the ritual, the steps are almost always the same.

PREPARATION
Start by clarifying your intention so your ritual has a focus, or a desired outcome. You'll need to think the ritual all the way through, to

make sure there's a clear beginning, middle, and end. The beginning is generally about setting sacred space, and calling in the forces; the middle is the enactment of the ritual; the ending brings closure.

Once you have a sense of the ritual, you can gather any objects and materials you will need, and find a location for it to occur. You will need to prepare the site of the ritual to ensure that there will be no surprises. Everything you need should be close at hand and in working order. During the ritual you want to clear the space of distractions as much as is possible.

Before you begin the actual ritual, you may want to prepare yourself in some way. This might include fasting, bathing, wearing a special amulet or a certain kind of clothing. Depending on the ritual, you might want to prepare yourself for several days, or for just a few minutes.

PROCESS
STEP 1. To begin the actual ritual, set up a sacred space. This might be as simple as shutting off the phone and closing the door to your room. Or it might mean creating a circle of rocks. Some people burn sage or incense to cleanse the energy around them. In ancient rituals, a circle was formed and the space outside the circle was swept clean, sealing the circle and creating a line of demarcation between that sacred space and the rest of the world.

STEP 2. Set your intention. You might do this aloud, silently, or in a symbolic way. If other people are involved, it's good to state aloud the purpose of the ritual, so that everyone's intention is aligned.

STEP 3. Call in the forces. This can be done through chanting, music, meditation, rattles, dancing, speaking a mantra, or any other way that seems right to you. Repetitive sounds or movement can help you to enter deeper and deeper into the energy of the ritual.

STEP 4. Begin the steps of the ritual, as you've outlined it, allowing yourself to surrender to it fully.

STEP 5. End the ritual. You can do this simply by blowing out a candle, placing the rocks from your circle back where you found them, or speaking words that give thanks and release the ritual. You might want to take a moment to open to appreciation for what has occurred.

CLOSURE

There are many ways to close a ritual. If many people are involved, this might be accomplished by people holding hands and singing a song, or by the facilitator saying a few words to thank everyone for participating, assuring them that their presence has been important and productive. If it has been an individual ritual, involving only you, you might want to spend some time journaling after the ritual is complete.

CORE TRIBAL PRACTICE SIX
MENTORING

INTRODUCTION

You can mentor someone in anything that you love to do and they wish to learn about. You can also be mentored by anyone who has wisdom or a skill to offer you. It often looks like the person being mentored is the one receiving all the value from the relationship. But we've found that the mentor also develops valuable skills and gets recognized for what they know. We hope you'll feel moved to try it.

FINDING A MENTOR

PREPARATION

Questions to explore when setting up a mentorship might include:

1. Is there someone in your life from whom you would like to learn, or whom you would like to teach?
2. Are your skill levels well matched with theirs? Could one of you be a good mentor, and the other a good student?

3. Do you both have the time and commitment to engage in this type of partnership?
4. Would you be willing to discuss your mutual concerns regarding mentorship?
5. What would you both gain from the mentorship?
6. Is this person an appropriate person for you to mentor, or be mentored by?
7. Does this mentorship complement or conflict with anything else the two of you are currently doing?

PROCESS

STEP 1. Clarify the commitment both individuals have to the mentorship. State the overall purpose of this relationship: what you each hope to gain from it, and what you will each offer to it. Be willing to make the mentorship a priority, and to learn from each other.

STEP 2. State the agreements necessary to support success. For example, how often will you communicate? What do you expect from each other between meetings, what kind of help is available? What are the time boundaries? What is the duration of the mentorship?

STEP 3. Assess the incoming skill level of the mentor and the student. Interview each other to make sure you don't begin your work together at a level that is too simplistic or too advanced.

STEP 4. Develop some learning objectives, or statements of specific, desired outcomes. Be as specific as possible, and include some way to assess what success would look like—how will you both know if you have achieved what you set out to accomplish?

STEP 5. Create an action plan which clarifies what you each will be doing, and in what time frame.

STEP 6. Define first steps and schedule your next contact. Don't underestimate the importance of beginning with a smooth, clear start; this gets the relationship started on the right foot!

STEP 7. Remember to check in from time to time to see how the process is going for both of you, how realistic the goals are, and what changes you might need to make in how you are working together.

You might want to enter into some mentorship relationships that are informal, and don't require this much set-up or ongoing attention. You can discuss this with the person you are mentoring, or being mentored by. Choose whatever level will work for you to accomplish your goals together.

CLOSURE

As you approach completion dates, check in with the person you're working with. Evaluate whether or not you will achieve the goals you established, if you should extend the time frame, or need to change something in the working relationship.

When you have completed your mentorship, you might want to share some kind of simple ritual that acknowledges or even celebrates this relationship. Rituals can be as simple as making up a certificate to present to the student, or having lunch together.

MENTORSHIP CIRCLES

A variation on one-on-one mentoring involves gathering in a circle, much like a council, but the purpose in this case is to let members of the tribe ask questions of each other, just for learning. These circles can be invaluable, as they promote open dialogue, and foster a rich sharing of knowledge and life experiences.

CORE TRIBAL PRACTICE SEVEN
SHARING SOUL WORK

INTRODUCTION

People love to be creative together, and soul work gives permission for this! We've found it quite powerful for people to come together to share their dreams, artwork, music, poetry, or dance. Soul work provides a structure for the sharing of imagination. This structure helps the tribe members to engage with one another, and allows members to be recognized for their creative expression, outside of the usual roles they play in life. We've found these times to be rich, inspiring, and incredibly moving. While there are many ways to share soul work, here are two specific ways that we have found work well.

DREAM CIRCLES

PREPARATION

When you're participating in a dream circle, set yourself up to record your dreams. We often imagine that we will simply remember our dreams, but upon waking they can elude us. Before going to sleep, put a pen and notepad beside your bed, or have a tape recorder handy. Have the first thing you do upon awakening be to ask yourself, "Did I dream?" Record any images, symbols, feelings, or impressions, no matter how small or seemingly insignificant.

Participating in a dream circle is valuable whether or not you have a dream to bring. The purpose of these circles is not to interpret or understand the dream, but instead, to witness and share their mystery.

PROCESS

STEP 1. Gather in groups of eight or less, sitting in a circle. While we have found four to six people to be ideal, you can do this with as few as two people.

STEP 2. Each person in the group has the opportunity to share a dream they had recently, or a dream they have remembered from the past that seems important to them. You might want to ask the dreamer to take a moment to close their eyes and imagine being in the dream again, then describe the dream as if it is happening the in present. For example, "As the dream begins I am standing on the seashore. Waves are lapping at my toes... shore birds are dancing up and down the wet sand..." It's helpful to remind the dreamer to speak slowly.

STEP 3. Ask the members of the circle to take time to listen openly and attentively to the dream.

STEP 4. Having heard the dream, the listeners might want to ask questions that draw out the dream and clarify it, as opposed to interpreting the dream. Examples of such questions might include:

Describe the time of day that the action in the dream took place. What did you feel as you were dreaming. Tell us more about one of the symbols, people, events. Did the dream stir up any memories, or give you any insights? What do you imagine the dream might be offering you? What was happening the day you had this dream? If the dream were posing a question to you, what would it be?

Dreams aren't problems to be solved, or puzzles to be understood. Instead of wrestling with a dream to see if you can "find out what it means," treat it gently, and just be open to any feelings, questions, or insights it might bring up for you.

STEP 5. Provide enough time that everyone who wants to offer a dream can do so, and do so without feeling rushed.

CLOSURE
Sharing our dreams is a private and intimate act. Ask each person to respect the sacredness of sharing and as they go out into the world to hold what they have witnessed here in confidence. If your group is working with journals, ask them to take a few moments to record anything that is meaningful for them.

LIVING MANDALA CIRCLES

INTRODUCTION
Like the sharing of dreams, mandala circles let us share that private and intimate inner world that is so important to us all. It is a wonderful celebration, and fosters heart connections that for many members of the tribe can last a lifetime.

PREPARATION
Ask tribe members to gather drawings, paintings, poetry, sculptures, or songs they have created, or which they would like to share and have witnessed. They might also wish to dance, share journal entries, photographs, or any other kind of creative or symbolic work.

PROCESS
STEP 1. Gather at a designated place, and arrange the artwork into a mandala. Pull the pieces in close to each other, making circles around circles of the artwork. You might want to play background music while creating the mandala. (We allow about twenty to thirty minutes from the time people start arriving for this.)

STEP 2. Once the mandala is made, allow time for tribe members to walk around the mandala, viewing it from all sides, taking it in as one whole piece of artwork that reflects the soul of the tribe.

STEP 3. Have the tribe members gather in a circle around the outside of the mandala, bringing their writings with them.

STEP 4. Depending on the size of the group, allow ample time for people to point out their artwork, talk about the process of making it, read their poetry or writings, dance, play instruments, sing songs, or say anything they would like. As in a council, people can speak as often as they want to, but the tribe should give no evaluation, critiques, or interpretations.

STEP 5. Be sure to give a five-minute warning when the time is coming to a close so that anybody who hasn't spoken, but who would like to, is offered one last chance.

CLOSURE
Sometimes it is best to close in silence. Other times we like to end by having open time for the tribe members to talk about whatever they are feeling from their experience of sharing this soul work.

CORE TRIBAL PRACTICE EIGHT
CREATING ALTARS

INTRODUCTION

Most of us already have altars in our homes, whether we are aware of them or not. These may be the shelves in our homes where we have pictures of people we love, objects with special meaning, important messages, or talismans that we consider good luck. For many, the mantle above a fireplace is the focal point of the room, holding objects with special meaning for those who make this place their home.

Carl Jung once said that if we each had a small altar to "source," our spiritual connection, no matter how small or how tucked away it was, it would remind us at an unconscious level, how we are part of a larger reality. Whether we spent daily time with the altar or not, it would quietly infuse our lives with meaning and connection with the invisible forces that sustain us.

Some people change their altars frequently, removing objects or bringing new ones in whenever it seems useful, or whenever they find a new object that inspires them. In this way, the altar can be a reminder of how one is changing and growing. Or the person may choose to keep on their altar only objects that he or she feels are changeless and eternal, such as a religious icon or a spiritual symbol.

Altars can be created for personal use, containing highly individualized objects, or for group use—for your family, project team, tribe, or any other group gathering.

PREPARATION

It could be said that the symbols we choose for an altar are the "gateless entrance" to a reality larger than ourselves. That's why it is so important to be clear about the purpose of your altar before you begin to create it. Select the objects for your altar on the basis of feelings they evoke for you. You might select objects that hold your personal intention, for example, the photo of a person who symbolizes an accomplishment or ideal toward which you're working. You might also include universal symbols, such as a tiny globe to symbolize the idea of oneness, or cultural symbols, such as a small artifact from the culture with which you most closely identify. You might include symbols of elemental energies such as wood and stones from the earth, a candle to symbolize fire, a feather or incense for air, or a small container or a shell to symbolize water. If you identify with Native American or Oriental traditions, you might include one or more statues or gemstones that symbolize healing, spiritual harmony or the creative force from those devotions. We have a friend who created a seasonal altar in her home, after she moved to a temperate climate. She had objects such as a pressed fall leaf from her home town, an empty robin's egg for spring, and a photo of a vibrant new rosebud for summer. When placed upon your altar, the objects you choose become the energetic building blocks to serve the purpose and intention of your altar.

PROCESS

STEP 1. Understand that your altar can serve any intention you desire. Take some time to focus your attention on what this might be. Here are a few possibilities:

- Anchoring a personal or professional goal or intention, such as starting your own business or buying a house.
- Keeping your heart and love open.
- Bringing new courage and self-trust.
- Establishing a firm grounding.
- Keeping connected to your family lineage, your spiritual traditions, or your religion.
- Holding thanks and giving gratitude for what you have.
- Asking for healing.

STEP 2. Choose a place to set up your altar. It might be a portion of a bookshelf in your living room, or a special shelf in your office or study. Gather the objects you have chosen and experiment with their placement in this location. You may find that some of the things you originally chose to place on your altar no longer seem appropriate, so just leave them out. Take your time setting up your altar. As our lives change, so do the objects and aspirations that we find meaningful.

STEP 3. The care and maintenance of your altar will depend on your personal relationship to it. Some people sit or stand before their altars at least once a day, using them as a focal point for prayer or meditation. Some people may only occasionally spend time at their altar, but in their minds it is always present, there to refer to whenever they desire.

CLOSURE

When is your altar complete? Our lives change, and with these changes we may discover new icons and symbols that inspire us. Try to create your altar in the spirit of leaving space for change and growth. At the same time, there are universal images and symbols that are eternal, that do not change—such as the belief that there are powers greater than ourselves. You may find yourself constantly searching for objects that you might add to your altar that best symbolize these.

CORE TRIBAL PRACTICE NINE
VOWS

INTRODUCTION

Vows are agreements that serve as the foundation for what is important to the tribe. This foundation enables you to take actions that support the health and well-being of the tribes you are involved with. Vows must reflect the tribe's common purpose and vision, and need to be reviewed periodically to keep them current. We have seen that the making and honoring of vows can prevent unspoken assumptions from creating problems and, when honored, are the tribe's solid foundation during challenging times. Vows work best when they are stated simply, and must be agreed on by all members involved.

PREPARATION

Before beginning to create any concrete vows, it's important to be sure that there is a common desire among all those involved to begin such a process. Once having established this, each person should spend time reflecting or journaling about what values, outcomes, and actions are important to them in this relationship.

PROCESS

STEP 1. Gather with the members of your tribe (remember, tribe is just another word for marriage, friendship, family, work group, community, neighborhood, etc.) and leave plenty of time to discuss the following questions. These questions will be much more helpful to you if you substitute for 'tribe' the specific relationship you're talking about, for example, marriage.

1. What are the main goals of this tribe?
2. What is your vision for this tribe now and over time?
3. To what is this tribe consecrated?
4. What are the values you want this tribe to express?
5. What are your secret hopes about how the members of this tribe will participate with each other?

It is important to set sacred space in some simple way (as we discussed earlier, in the section about ritual) before you enter into these conversations.

STEP 2. Take the answers to these questions and try to form a few statements that capture the most important values of the tribe. For example, a work group might take a vow to respect each other's ideas and communicate honestly with each other; a family might vow to appreciate each other's differences and hold each other in love; a couple might vow to bring their maturity and openness to each other, or to use the relationship to learn to love again and again.

STEP 3. Once the vows are mutually agreed on, it is useful to do a simple ritual of having the members of the tribe speak the vows to each other.

STEP 4. Be sure to decide how often you will review these vows.

For Couples—Use these questions to reflect on what your marriage is about. You might want to do a yearly review and renewal of your vows.

For Companies—Use these questions to assist a work group with establishing the agreements they will need to make and keep with each other to meet their goals and stay "on the same page." This is best done when a new project begins, though any time is better than not at all. The agreements can be reviewed monthly, or midway through the project.

CLOSURE

Give a quick summary of the vows as you understand them. If you have established a time to re-examine and restate your vows, as described in Step 4, be sure to include this in your summary.

CORE TRIBAL PRACTICE TEN
PRAYER

INTRODUCTION

Prayer is the vehicle through which we can petition life's unseen forces. Prayer is available to everyone, regardless of religious preference, and isn't only for times of crisis. Through prayer, the tribe has the opportunity to join together in common purpose and love.

There is much empirical evidence suggesting that prayer is one of the ways we can effect change in our lives. In recent years, medical research has shown that distant prayer, and even prayer where the recipient is unaware of people praying for them, can have a positive healing effect on a person's health.

We've found that when our tribe comes together in prayer they are always moved by it, and they invariably leave feeling enriched and inspired by the experience.

PREPARATION

Whether in individual or group prayer, it's a good idea to establish a sacred space, that is, a time and place where you will not be disturbed. Take a moment to still your mind, and focus on feelings of acceptance, openness, and love.

PROCESS

PERSONAL PRAYER

Depending on your religious traditions or spiritual practices, you may have your own way of praying. If you already follow a particular practice that's comfortable for you, you might want to ignore the following. If you don't already have a method of prayer, you may find the following guidelines helpful:

STEP 1. Begin with a brief period of silence, perhaps following a meditation.

STEP 2. Focus your attention on an image or feeling of eternal spirit that is familiar to you.

STEP 3. Now state your prayer, either aloud or inwardly, feeling your connection with spirit as you do. Hold this prayer softly in your heart, asking that this prayer be heard and answered.

STEP 4. Close the prayer by giving thanks.

GROUP PRAYER

Whenever a tribe gathers, the group can simply take a bit of time for anyone to speak aloud the name of someone for whom they desire a group prayer. Or they may ask for prayers to honor or support any endeavor, such as world peace, or for healing for an individual or group facing a crisis.

CLOSURE
After praying and giving thanks, again observe a moment of silence before going onto other business.

II

GETTING STARTED: FAMILY, COMMUNITY, WORKPLACE, INTIMACY, SELF

IN FAMILY

STORYTELLING. Once a month, gather together and tell events from your life as stories. Let everyone participate. Possible topics include:

- Stories about your family history.
- Times someone was inspired or in awe of life.
- Stories from the week.

Another fun way to use storytelling is to create a group story. One person starts and tells a story for a minute or two, and then the next person picks it up and keeps adding to and creating it.

CREATE BIRTHDAY RITUALS. Using the building blocks for ritual, create birthday rituals that might include the following:

- The person whose birthday it is says what they are grateful for in their life.
- Those gathered for the celebration tell why they are grateful that the birthday person was born.
- The person whose birthday it is makes a gift for the family to thank them for the support and love he or she has received during the year.
- Each family member gives the birthday person a gift that symbolizes the hopes and dreams they have for them for the coming year.

FAMILY COUNCILS. Possible topics include:

- What it feels like to be you in the family.
- If you could change places with anyone in the family, who would it be and why?
- What you like, appreciate, and admire about each other and the family as a whole.
- What each family member is currently learning about themselves and life.
- How each family member learns best and what kinds of things motivate them.

CREATE RITUALS for the seasons, holidays, personal transitions, or to simply begin each meal you have together.

SOUL WORK. Designate a period of time to come together and do soul work. Each family member can work in the medium they enjoy the most. You might paint, work with clay, play music, or write poetry. If you want, you might take time to share what you have created.

CREATE A FAMILY VISION AND GOALS. Come together as a family to discuss your vision for the next two years, and once you have, look through magazines and photos to create a poster that reflects those goals and vision. Hang the poster in your home, where everyone can see it every day. A variation of this exercise asks each family member to share their individual two-year vision for themselves.

MAKE A FAMILY ALTAR. Families can have an altar to which each member contributes. The altar might symbolize:

- Your love and commitment to each other.
- Your common spiritual beliefs.

- Your family lineage, with pictures of your ancestors.
- Your vows or family vision.

The family might want to change the altar during different seasons, or make it special in some way during holiday times, for birthdays, important milestones, or when a family member is ill or needs special attention.

Keep the altar simple, using pictures, symbols, and objects you love. Share the meaning of each object, and make this a "living" altar. Change it as often as you desire.

FAMILY RECOGNITIONS: You can use the following format for offering family recognitions:

Give specific, verbal recognitions to each other such as:

"I appreciate you for _____."
"What I have been learning from you this month is _____."
"I am aware that you are working really hard at _____ for our family."

STAND IF YOU... Gather with your extended family and do this exercise. Sample questions might include:

- Stand if you were born in a foreign country.
- Stand if you have a college degree.
- Stand if you play a musical instrument.
- Stand if you like to dance.
- Stand if you're feeling unappreciated.
- Stand if you feel successful in your life now.

Questions can be anything you would like to know about each other.

MENTOR EACH OTHER. Have siblings mentor other siblings, sons mentor fathers, grandparents with grandchildren, in any area they feel they have something to offer each other, or would most want to learn from each other. This could be mentoring on anything from cooking, to how to be playful and light, to sportsmanship. Change partners or roles every one to three months.

IN COMMUNITY

FOOD. Plant and tend a communal garden. Once every two weeks get together, cook a big pot of food, and send the food home with each family.

COUNCILS. Do a multi-generational council: Gather in groups of men and women ranging in age from their twenties through their sixties. The group is split in two—people ages twenty to thirty-nine, and people ages forty and older. Each group listens to the other's council. Council topics that work well include:

> Round 1: Discuss the most valuable time period of your life, what made it valuable for you, and what it brought you.
> Round 2: What do you consider the biggest failure of your life? What was it like for you? What counsel would you give others in a similar situation?
> Round 3: What are your hopes and dreams for your life right now?

Using the same format as the multi-generational council, gather a group of men and women and first have a council of women listening to men, and then have the men listening to the women answer the following questions:

> Round 1: What do you love about being a man (woman)?
> Round 2: What do you want men or women to know about you as a man (woman)?

Round 3: What do you love, admire, and respect about men (women)?

Round 4: What do you fear about men (women)?

Additional council topics for communities can include:

- Women talking about child raising, with pregnant women listening.
- Newly divorced men and women council with remarried men and women.
- Grief councils, for anyone suffering any kind of loss.

RITUALS

- Divorce rituals for the community to witness and receive you as a separate individual once again.
- Retirement rituals to honor the achievements and milestones of your career, and to open to the new, unknown life that lies ahead.
- Menstruation rituals to celebrate a young woman's coming into her power, and to honor her body.
- Rituals that mark the passage from child to adult. Honoring the young adult's new capacity, budding maturity. Recognizing the change for the family members whose lives are also changing as a result of this passage.
- Letting-go and death rituals to allow community members who are grieving know they are supported in their grief. Have them be witnessed as they release the person or thing in their life that has ended or died.
- New Year's—celebrating the release of the old and ushering in the new.
- Thanksgiving—celebrating what each tribe member is thankful for.
- Rites of Spring—celebrating new life, new goals, or anything emergent.

STORYTELLING. Possible topics include:

- Stories about the funniest moment of your life.
- Stories about a time in your life you were inspired.
- Women gather to share their labor stories with pregnant women or one another.
- Groups gather at community centers to tell stories of times they experienced a moment of grace, or connection with the mystery of life.
- Fathers and mothers gather to share moments in their lives they have loved parenting.
- Grandparents gather to tell stories about their grandchildren, and their treasured experiences of grand parenting.

MAKE IT A PERSONAL PRACTICE to teach one thing to someone everyday. Ask to be taught something by someone in your community.

ONCE A MONTH look to see what your community needs and how you can be of service to it. Make it a practice to offer your help or support to someone each day. Gift something you value on a regular basis: your time, money, an object, etc.

DO THE "STAND IF YOU..." EXERCISE. Possible groupings and questions include:

Groups of men and women:

- Stand if you have ever been in the Armed Forces.
- Stand if your father has died.
- Stand if you have children (Stay standing if you have more than 1 child, more than 2, etc.).
- Stand if you have sisters but no brothers.
- Stand if you work for yourself.
- Stand if you have ever been fired.

- Stand if you have ever lived alone (Stay standing if you have ever lived alone for 5 years or more, 7 years or more, etc.).

In a local community center, church group, or neighborhood:

- Stand if you love gardening.
- Stand if you have a pet.
- Stand if you love to play sports or an instrument (you can list them).
- Stand if you are interested in computers.
- Stand if you have ever had a serious illness.
- Stand if you love to travel.
- Stand if both of your parents have died.

Groups of parents:

- Stand if you have teenagers.
- Stand if you want to have more children.
- Stand if you ever feel overwhelmed with child raising.
- Stand if you have the pressures of a two-income home.
- Stand if your extended family lives out of town.
- Stand if you have a special needs child.
- Stand if you were an only child.

MENTORSHIP CIRCLES. Some examples include:

- Young people asking the elders about aging.
- Those about to go to college asking what it is like to be in a university.
- Community members asking those with illness what it's like.
- New parents seeking advice from experienced parents.

RECOGNITION. Neighborhood or community groups can work with recognition in several ways. Here are three:

- Designate one night every few months to come together and do Living Mandala circles.
- Offer each other verbal recognitions such as, "What I see you bring to this group is _____," or, "You've contributed to our group through _____," or, "What I appreciate about you is _____."
- Gather monthly or quarterly for dream work circles.

PRAYER CIRCLES. Gather with friends, temple or church groups, or with your neighbors for prayer. During times of social crisis, offer unconditional love regardless of the specific politics or outcomes, that somehow the crisis may turn out for the collective good. Or, whenever a group is gathered, take the time to find out if anyone wants the group's prayers for themselves or someone else in their lives. Additionally, you may want to gather on the winter and summer solstices and during other important times of year.

IN THE WORKPLACE

CREATE RITUALS FOR:

- Celebrating someone's promotion.
- Marking and recognizing a team's success.
- Setting in motion the intention of a new project.
- Signifying the beginning and ending of a meeting.

FIND A MENTOR.

Mentors may be people who have successfully completed the type of project or job you are currently working on, or people who are in positions that you aspire to at work. They may also be people who handle themselves professionally in a way you respect and would want to learn. Use the same criteria to decide to whom to offer yourself as a mentor.

Interview someone who has a skill set you need, or who has accomplished something you wish to learn. Find out all you can about how they achieved what they did. Offer to do this for someone who wishes to learn from you.

FIND FIVE PEOPLE to give you positive encouragement and feedback each day for one week, and offer to do the same for them.

DO "STAND IF YOU..." with an existing work group to help them get to know each other, or to assist with building trust. Questions you can use include:

- Stand if you have ever managed more than five people.
- Stand if you are sole income provider in your family.
- Stand if you have a Master's Degree.
- Stand if you ever accomplished something professionally that seemed impossible.

COUNCILS. Possible groupings are senior managers with line managers, people across divisions, the executive leadership team, etc.

Topics for discussion could include:

- Major career obstacles that were overcome.
- The challenges of balancing personal goals with career goals.
- A time you failed in your career, and what you learned.
- Sharing how key wins have been accomplished.
- The most challenging moment of your career.
- A vision you have for your job and work.
- The challenges of balancing personal achievement and the empowerment of others.

A group of people from different divisions but with similar job roles and tasks might hold a council on what they are doing that is particularly effective.

STORYTELLING. Some suggestions for topics:

- Senior management share success stories with new hires.
- Senior management gather to share the stories of their rise to position in the corporation with new hires.
- People who have worked in the company for a long time gather with the staff to tell stories of the company's history.
- People gather across divisions to tell "war stories" of the year (times that were difficult, but where they persevered.)

ALTARS. Work teams create an altar in a central location, holding objects representing the collective goals, symbols of project milestones, and the teams' hopes for success. They might want to change the altar during different stages of the project to reflect the changing needs of the team.

VOWS. Use the questions in Chapter 10 to help your work group establish those mutual agreements which you will need to make and keep in order to meet your goals and stay "on the same page." Making agreements is best done when a new project begins, though any time is better than not at all. The agreements can be reviewed monthly, or midway through the project.

MENTORSHIP CIRCLES. Managers gather with the people who directly report to them to ask the following types of questions:

- How do you like to be managed?
- What motivates you?
- What situations are particularly stressful for you?

Their direct reports might want to ask questions to their managers such as:

- How can we more effectively communicate?
- What is it like to manage us?

Both groups might ask and answer the following:

- What do you need to be more effective?
- What types of things are frustrating to you?
- What types of things already work well?

Experienced managers can work with new hires or newly promoted managers to answer questions about performance reviews, how to say no to employees, typical situations they can expect to face, or to give tips for success on effectiveness.

People with similar job functions across the organization could come together in a mentorship circle for collective problem solving. It's very effective when the senior leadership of an organization does this too!

RECOGNITION

Yearly awards are offered based on an employee vote. Categories might include awards for individual results and achievement or individual contributions to the betterment of the corporate culture.

You can also create organizational recognition by using the "Stand if you..." exercise on an annual basis. Gather the whole company or division in a room and ask questions like:

- Stand if you took on more responsibility this year.
- Stand if you achieved something this year that seemed out of your reach last year.
- Stand if you are learning a new skill set.

IN INTIMATE RELATIONSHIPS

COUNCILS ON:

- What you most love about the relationship.
- What you each long for in the relationship.

- What you each vision for your lives in five, ten and twenty years.
- The ways in which you're different now than when you first met.

MENTOR EACH OTHER. It can often be wonderful to mentor or be mentored by your partner in an area where they are accomplished, or in one they simply enjoy. Choose something you'd like to share more deeply with your partner. Examples include cooking, gardening, working with computers, playing a sport (or just being a good spectator), how to play a musical instrument, antiquing, how to play the stock market, or something related to your profession.

VOWS. Use the questions offered earlier in Chapter 10 to reflect on what your relationship is about. You might want to do a yearly review and renewal of these vows.

CREATE AN ALTAR. You can create many different kinds of altars for your relationship, containing objects and pictures you have gathered separately or together. The intention of the altar can vary widely. For example, you could have:

- A soul work altar.
- An altar to remind you of your vows to each other.
- An altar to hold your long-term goals and visions together.
- An altar simply dedicated to your love.

You may want to add to or change the altar a few times each year, or during important transitions.

OFFERING RECOGNITIONS. Come together one evening a week and offer each other recognitions. For example, "What I value that you bring to us is _____," and, "What I appreciate about how you are with me is _____."

JOIN WITH OTHER COUPLES IN STORYTELLING CIRCLES

to share about topics such as how you handle your money, how you resolve conflict, and vacations or trips you have taken that you love.

PRAYER.

Come together during a designated, quiet time, and ask each other to pray for something specific, pray for something you want in your relationship, or share the prayers that you have in your hearts for each other and your relationship. During difficult times, you might want to ask your families or communities to pray for you.

SOUL WORK.

Spend time together in the same room doing art-work, writing poetry, or playing a musical instrument. You might want to share your work at the end of the evening. You could create a piece of soul work to exchange with each other that, for example, expresses how you feel about the relationship. You might also wish to create a piece of soul work together.

DO SOMETHING FOR YOUR PARTNER

without being asked to. Do something you know they really love, or is really important to them. Give them an object of yours that you really value, to take with them when you're away from each other.

SPEAK YOUR DREAMS

to each other on a regular basis. You may want to refer to some of the questions we have offered in the previous chapter to help each other clarify your dreams.

WITH YOURSELF

BUILD ALTARS FOR:

- What you love.
- Your hopes and aspirations.
- Life passages (pictures and symbols of yourself at each age and stage).
- Your ancestors (pictures and symbols from your lineage).

JOURNAL (keep it as simple as ten minutes each day).

- Keep a daily-life reflections journal to give to your children when they're grown. Let them read who you were, and they'll better see who you are.
- Keep a self-recognition journal. Each day list five things you did well, or when you were courageous, or took a risk.
- Keep a dream journal.

ONCE A WEEK ASK YOURSELF, "What is a neglected part of myself this week?" and do something to honor that part.

TAKE ONE HOUR A WEEK FOR YOURSELF, with no planned activity or goal.

TAKE ONE HOUR A WEEK FOR SOUL WORK. Do unstructured art, clay, dance, singing, or any other form of creative expression.

PRACTICE ASKING YOURSELF, "Who's talking?" Did you just hear your inner child, warrior, critic, wisdom voice? Who is talking?

TAKE A DREAM SYMBOL or image and concretize it. Make it real and concrete by drawing, painting, sculpting, or journaling with it.

EACH MORNING TAKE A MOMENT to pay attention to your breath and to give thanks for life (regardless of how your life feels at that moment.)

EACH MORNING READ ONE LINE FROM A BOOK OR POETRY COLLECTION that moves or inspires you. Keep that feeling close to you each day. Work a poem: Choose a poem that you love and slowly weave it into the fabric of your life. Memorize it. Say it to yourself each day, and practice seeing your life through this poem. Work the poem for many months and then choose a new one.

MAKE A FEW SIMPLE agreements with yourself and keep them.

12

EPILOGUE

WITHIN THE Zen Buddhist tradition there is a series of ten woodcuts, delineating the age-old path of conscious awakening. The first woodcut begins with an ordinary, everyday scene. A man is standing in the marketplace and, as he looks down, he sees the footprints of an ox (which in this tradition symbolizes God, the Transcendent). His eyes follow these footprints, and he sees them leading out of the marketplace. Somehow, he has been called away from ordinary life. In the next woodcut, he honors the call and follows the footprints away from the market, away from his life as he has known it, out and into the fields.

The subsequent six woodcuts show the man in his approach to God. We see him trembling with awe and fear, wrestling with the ox, kneeling in supplication. We see him learn to approach the ox, making peace with his fear and taming the ox. We see him get up on the ox, and in the seventh woodcut he joins in full communion and celebration with the ox, having ridden him home. In the eighth woodcut man and ox are depicted as disappearing into transcendent union together. They have become one.

But the story doesn't end here.

The ninth woodcut shows the man in the field, the sun shining, the ox gone, and he sees footprints leading back toward the marketplace. In the tenth and final woodcut, the man has followed those footprints back to the very marketplace where his journey began. He has returned to his ordinary life, to the life of his tribe and community, but something has changed. Everywhere he looks, in all the stands and fruit stalls, in all the trees and gardens, everything is blooming! He is back in his everyday life, yet he carries with him the experience of the sacred, and with that, ordinary life comes alive![1]

The practices in this book take us on the same journey, from the ordinary lives that we each lead into a connection with the sacred through tribal consciousness. Just as our man in the Zen woodcut returns to the marketplace with a new consciousness, the question for us is, can we bring our connection to the sacred into the most ordinary realms of our daily existence? The answer is yes. We have seen it day after day, in thousands of people's lives, over the past eleven years. We have seen ordinary families, communities, workplaces, and homes begin to bloom, becoming richer and more fully alive.

The last two Zen woodcuts speak to a changing world consciousness. It is no longer enough for the spiritual path to be available only by leaving our lives. With modern technology breaking down walls, partitions, and boundaries, there comes a pressing urge for us to wake up, to enter a world re-visioned, to embrace a new value system.

Our challenge is to participate in the re-creation of sacred tribal values, to become world tribe members, to choose to live with modern tribal values. Everywhere we turn we see that tribal renewal is already occurring: the AIDS Quilt project, movie stars giving their time and energy to fundraise for important projects, the fundamentalist movement, the increase of cults. We know tribal renewal is emerging as we see New Age gurus entering the White House, see new book titles with the words "Soul" and "Spirit" in stores every day, hear keynote speakers at corporate conferences delivering talks on "Spirit in the Workplace."

What drives all of this is the collective longing for connection. Like tender new shoots just breaking through the soil in spring, our changes in consciousness start small. But if we nurture them, they'll grow.

One year when we had taken a small group to Bali, a group member named Sarah became mildly ill. I (Carole) asked in the village where the nearest healer was, and we were sent to the village priest. He agreed to work on Sarah, and asked the rest of the group to please have a seat in the courtyard, and to prepare ourselves for ritual. A few moments later his wife returned and ushered us into the inner courtyard. We sat in rows, facing the Hindu/Animist altar to Shiva, Brahma, and Vishnu. The altar was beautiful. Incense was burning, and there were flower offerings everywhere. The water to be used as holy water had been blessed and infused with rose petal essence, and there was sweet sticky rice to use in the ceremony.

I closed my eyes, and as I began my meditation, I became aware of many other sounds and activities around me. A dog came up and licked my face. Children laughed and played next to our ceremonial mat, as I heard the priest pick up his bells to call in the forces for the ritual. I also heard the sounds of pots clanking as evening meals were being prepared, and arguments happening far off in the distant neighborhood. At first I was annoyed—didn't this priest and his family understand that we were entering ritual? But slowly I became aware of another feeling... one of grace. Life was happening all around us, real life, beautiful, delicious, simple, ordinary life. And at the same time, so was our ritual. I felt such gratitude, and at the same time I felt grief. Gratitude that I could be sitting here in Bali and know that, somewhere in the world, the sacred and the ordinary life was being lived together, as it had been for hundreds of years. That here, in this village, nothing was excluded. The children growing up in this man's household would know that the sacred is interwoven with the profane, that life holds it all. And I felt grief that my own son would not live in such wholeness. Not yet. But someday, perhaps his son will.

In Western culture the sacred is housed in buildings far away from ordinary, day-to-day events. No wonder we have to make ritual such a big deal—it rarely happens. Our yearning for sacred tribal process within our daily lives can be seen in our restlessness and our relentless quests. But what we're searching for is right in front of us. The renewal of sacred tribal consciousness won't happen all at once. It can't. But it takes just one person to begin practicing in one place; one person to reach their hand out to another and say "I know you." We have traveled the world and discovered that everywhere people are waiting to be seen, recognized, and valued. You could be the one person in your community who sees the footprints lead to a new direction, and you could have the courage to follow them.

We have so few real, initiatory tribal gatherings available to us. It's no wonder that street gangs spring up and grow. Gangs are one avenue for our youth to experience tribal participation in a modern society, albeit not the best way!

There's a story about a Swiss physicist who collected pendulums. One day he decided to paint his home. He gathered all of his pendulums and placed them together in one room. After the paint was dry in the rest of the house, he came back into the room, intent on returning the pendulums to their original positions. He discovered that they were all moving in sync! Being the curious scientist that he was, he wanted to discover with which pendulum they had come into alignment, so he set about finding out. He started each of the pendulums at different rates and at different times, measured them each day, and began to discover that all of the pendulums were aligning themselves with the pendulum of the greatest mass. It wasn't the largest pendulum; it was a smaller one. But it carried the greatest weight.

This story is significant. We have entered a time that needs, if not a new religious order, a new religious attitude. An attitude of worship, devotion, attention to the heart. An attitude of searching for the mature self. How can I participate fully in life? In what ways can I contribute? What is life asking of me? How can I take my place in my tribe?

It takes a new, living consciousness to shift our current one. It doesn't happen all at once, but like the pendulums, the new consciousness must gather mass. This occurs slowly. But over time, as we sow the seeds of tribe, tribal renewal will happen. We could have written volumes in the how-to section about any one of the practices: dream work, soul work, meditation. We began with what we feel to be intrinsic, simple ways to practice, things that can easily be done. We hope that you will practice the tribal values in some way each day.

Max Zeller, in memory of C. G. Jung, writes about a dream he had once related to Jung, and Jung's comments about it in 1949.

And this was my dream:

A temple of vast dimensions was in the process of being built. As far as I could see—ahead, behind, right and left—there were incredible numbers of people building on gigantic pillars. I too was building on a pillar. The whole building process was in its very first beginning, but the foundation was already there, the rest of the building was starting to go up, and I and many others were working on it.

Jung said, "Ja, you know, that is the temple we all build on. We don't know the people because, believe me, they build in India, and China, and in Russia, and all over the world. That is the new religion. You know how long it will take until it is built?"

I said, "How should I know? Do you know?"

He said "I know. About six hundred years."

"Where do you know this from?" I asked.

He said, "From dreams. From other people's dreams and my own. This new religion will come together as far as we can see."[2]

We live in extraordinary times. The revitalization and re-emergence of tribal consciousness is necessary. We have to value our lives, and offer them to our tribes. As we begin, we build on the temple.

As Max Zeller said:

"Each person works on his own pillar, until one day the temple will be built."

Carole Kammen and Jodi Gold
Summer, 1997

NOTES

PART I: INTRODUCTION

1. Visit our web site at www.onetribe.com to find plans for monthly tribal gatherings, locations of groups near you, and guidelines for starting your own groups, as well as materials and products you can order.

2. E. S. Craighill and Mary Kawena Pukui, *The Polynesian Family System in Ka-'u, Hawaii*. Boston: Charles E. Tuttle, Co., Inc., 1991.

CHAPTER 2

1. Caryn Lea Summers, *Circle of Health: Recovery Through the Medicine Wheel,* Freedom, CA: The Crossing Press, 1991, 8.

CHAPTER 5

1. Diane K. Osborn (Ed.). *A Joseph Campbell Companion: Reflections of the Art of Living*, New York: Harper Collins, 1991.

CHAPTER 6

1. Alice Walker, from an interview about her work in *Common Boundary* magazine, 1991.
2. Rainer Maria Rilke, *Letters to a Young Poet,* translated by M.D. Herter Norton, New York: W.W. Norton, 1934.

CHAPTER 8

1. Carl G. Jung, *Memories, Dreams, Reflections*, New York: Vintage, 1965, 252.
2. Jung, *Memories, Dreams, Reflections*, 252.
3. Jung, *Memories, Dreams, Reflections*, 253.
4. Carl G. Jung, *Man and His Symbols*, New York: Dell, 1968.
5. N. B. Stone and P. Hart (Eds.) *Thomas Merton: Love and Living*, New York: Bantam, 1979.
6. This is an interpretation of several different manuscripts by Hal Zina Bennett.
7. Max Zeller, adapted from a story told to him by Carl Jung. Published by the Analytical Psychology Club of San Francisco, CA, 1961.

Chapter 9

1. To read more about the Fuegan story, see: *Rhythms of Vision* by Lawrence Blair, New York: Schocken Books, 1976.

2. China Galland, *Longing for Darkness*, New York: Penguin, 1990.

3. Paul Seaman. This poem is excerpted from Paul Seaman's *Paper Airplanes in the Himalayas: The Unfinished Path Home,* South Bend, IN: CrossCultural Publications, Inc., 1997. Available from the author for $22.50 (post paid), 19101 Broadwater Way, Gaithersburg, MD 20879-2167; (301) 963-8087.

Chapter 12 – Epilogue

1. If you want to read more about the Zen Woodcut story, see: *Zen Flesh, Zen Bones,* compiled by Paul Reps and Nyogen Senzaki, Boston: Shambhala, 1994.

2. Max Zeller, as quoted in the Analytical Psychology Club of San Francisco, CA, 1961.

BIBLIOGRAPHY

Bergson, Henri. *The Comic Ethic.* (Essay translated by Arthur Mitchell, N.p., 1944).

Blair, Lawrence. *Rhythms of Vision.* New York: Schocken Books, 1976.

Campbell, Joseph. *Myths to Live By.* New York: Penguin Books, 1993.

Campbell, Joseph, Moyers, William & Flowers, Betty Sue. *The Power of Myth.* New York: Doubleday, 1988.

Channing, William Ellery. *The Union.* N.p., 1829.

Channing, William Ellery. *Complete Works.* N.p., 1879.

Duerk, Judith. *Circle of Stones.* San Diego, CA: LuraMedia, 1989.

Edinger, Edward F. *The Creation of Consciousness.* Toronto: Inner City Books, 1984.

Einstein, Albert. *What I Believe.* N.p., 1930.

Eiseman, Fred B., Sr. *Bali: Sekala and Niskala.* N.p.: Periplus Editions, 1989.

Galland, China. *Longing For Darkness.* New York: Penguin, 1990.

Handy, E.S. Craighill, and Mary Kawena Pukui. *The Polynesian Family System in Ka-'u, Hawaii.* Boston: Charles E. Tuttle, Co., Inc., 1991.

Johnson, Robert. *Inner Work.* San Francisco: HarperSanFrancisco, 1989.

Johnson, Robert. *Owning Your Own Shadow.* SanFrancisco: HarperSanFrancisco, 1993.

Jung, Carl. *The Collected Works of C.G. Jung, #5: Symbols of Transformation.* Princeton, NJ: Princeton University Press, 1967.

Jung, Carl. *Man and his Symbols.* New York: Dell, 1968.

Jung, Carl. *Memories, Dreams, Reflections.* New York: Vintage Books, 1965.

Katz, Richard. *Boiling Energy: Community Healing Among the Kalahari Kung.* Boston: Harvard University Press, 1984.

Lichtheim, Miriam (Translation of Chapter 1). *The Instruction of Amenemope.* N.p., n.d.

Miller, Henry. *Tropic of Cancer.* New York: Grove Press, 1989.

Mitchell, Stephen. *The Selected Poetry of Rainer Maria Rilke.* New York: Vintage Books, 1989.

Mitchell, Stephen. *The Enlightened Heart.* New York: Harper & Row, 1993.

Moore, Thomas. *Care of the Soul.* New York: HarperCollins, 1994.

Moyne, Buhn and Coleman Barks. *Open Secret: Versions of Rumi.* Putney, VT: Threshold Books, 1984.

O'Brien, Justin. (Editor & Translator). *Maxims of Marcel Proust.* N.p., 1948.

Osborn, Diane K. (Ed.). *A Joseph Campbell Companion: Relections of the Art of Living.* New York: Harper Collins, 1991.

Perera, Sylvia Brinton. *Descent to the Goddess.* Toronto: Inner City Books, 1989.

Reps, Paul and Nyogen Senzaki (Compilers). *Zen Flesh, Zen Bones.* Boston: Shambhala, 1994.

Richards, Mary Caroline. *The Crossing Point.* Middletown, CT: Wesleyan University Press, 1973.

Rilke, Rainer Maria. *Letters to a Young Poet.* Translated by M.D. Herter Norton, New York: W.W. Norton, 1934.

Seaman, Paul. *Paper Airplanes in the Himalayas: The Unfinished Path Home.* South Bend, IN: Cross Cultural Publications, Inc., 1997.

Somé, Malidoma. *Of Water and the Spirit.* New York: Penguin, 1995.

Stone, N.B. and P. Hart (Eds.). *Thomas Merton: Love and Living.* New York: Bantam, 1979.

Summers, Caryn Lea. *Circle of Health: Recovery Through the Medicine Wheel.* Freedom, CA: The Crossing Press, 1991.

Van der Post, Laurens. *Venture to the Interior.* New York: Harcourt Brace, 1979.

Woodman, Marion. *The Pregnant Virgin.* Toronto: Inner City Books, 1985.

Woodman, Marion. *Leaving My Father's House.* Boston: Shambhala, 1993.

Zeller, Max. "Memories of Jung." Article printed in a booklet published by the Analytical Psychology Club of San Francisco, 1961.

Voices of the Tribe

Our heart-felt thanks to the members of our tribe who have so generously shared their lives, their words, and their wisdom with us. Their contributions are the real life stories, poems and memories included in this book.

Angeli Achatz
Leigh Alexander
Hank Atkins
Greg Baker
Bob & Hilary Beban
Tina Benson
Rachel Carpenter
Barbara Clark
Jan Cohn
Diana Everline
Virginia M. Fleming
Jerry Fox
Rick Garza
Kitt Goldberg
Ned Gorman
Deborah Heller
Ralph Hoar
Sollace Hotze
Mark Hulbert
Marcus Jung
Kimberly Lopes
Wallace Mann
Bruce McDiffett
Chrissa Merron
Lily Myers
Heidi Pandula
Christopher Rosebrook
Paul Seaman
Jan Smith
Richard Whiteley
Kevin Wrathall

CAROLE KAMMEN, co-founder of The Pathways Institute, is a visionary lecturer in the field of transformational arts. She also provides consulting and mentorship for individual clients and corporations.

JODI GOLD, co-owner of The Pathways Institute, specializes in group process and curriculum design. Jodi uses her skill as an educator to create dynamic and powerful learning environments.

The authors have traveled widely, participating in cultures where tribal relationship is still alive and vital. In their work, co-directing the Pathways Institute, they have created a challenging and nurturing environment in which to address fundamental relationships to Self, to Life, and to Others. Carole and Jodi have made a unique contribution to the human potential movement by bringing the ancient philosophies into contemporary life.

Over 10,000 people have graduated from The Pathways Institute during the last eleven years. Their graduates come from a wide range of backgrounds and businesses, including: Industrial Light and Magic, Lucasfilm, Oracle, Charles Schwab, the Fidelity Corp., MCI, Levi Strauss, US Dept. of Commerce, Stanford Business School, and many others.

JODI GOLD   CAROLE KAMMEN

The Pathways Institute is a modern day Mystery School which teaches the skills that lead to inner knowledge and personal development. The Institute offers a challenging and nurturing environment in which to address fundamental relationships to Self, to Life, and to Others.

Our workshops, training programs, travel retreats, community gatherings, and tribal celebrations guide individuals in developing the skills for realizing their own goals and dreams.

In addition to our foundational studies, the Institute also includes a four-year curriculum in the sacred arts, and a corporate training division, offering leadership and management training and customized consulting.

To find out about The Pathways Institute's programs and communities, write to:

The Pathways Institute
7 Mt. Lassen Drive, Suite C258
San Rafael, California 94903

or e-mail us at:

info@PathwaysInstitute.com

About www.onetribe.com

CHECK OUR WEB SITE TO:

- Connect to World Wide Tribal Gatherings

- Find out about how others are putting the Sacred Tribal Values into practice

- Share successful ideas about how you are utilizing the Sacred Tribal Values in your home, workplace, community, or with yourself

- Order audio tapes and other educational materials

ABOUT THE NAME *PATHWAYS INSTITUTE*

The Pathways Institute was formerly known as Temenos Associates, Inc., a national teaching organization specializing in consciousness work, personal growth and the sacred arts. Temenos Associates, Inc. was not affiliated with Temenos®, Inc., recognized for the development of win-win interpersonal relationships and organizational cultures.

Audio Tapes Available from OneTribe

Sacred Connection Meditations© have been developed and created by authors and teachers, Carole Kammen and Jodi Gold, co-directors of Pathways Institute.

SACRED CONNECTION WITH THE HEART

This tape features a 20-minute guided meditation that you can use daily to renew and nourish your heart center, and to access the qualities of harmony, compassion and unconditional love. As you practice this meditation over time, you will develop resources that bring balance, wholeness and healing into your life. This tape includes an introduction to the heart center and its attributes, as well as simple steps for meditating.

CREATING INNER CONNECTIONS: *Sacred Circle Meditation & Embracing the Ancestors Meditation*

The *Sacred Circle* provides a daily meditation for contemplation and awakening. You can use this meditation to open to a quiet inner place for prayer, renewal, healing or to seek counsel and guidance. *Embracing the Ancestors* is a deeply personal journey into your inner world, guiding you to connect with sacred space and to open to ancestral wisdom available to us all. Receive the blessings, energies and love of your ancestors.

SACRED CONNECTION WITH LIFE: *Overview of Life Meditation & Inspiration Meditation*

Overview of Life offers an opportunity for you to take stock of your life, in an open, non-judgmental way. In this meditation you will step back from your day-to-day life and gain a fresh, new perspective. Drawing upon the discoveries you have made, you may use the *Inspriration Meditation* to infuse your life today with vision and renewed inspiration. Gain clarity and discernment about your life and any choices you might be making. These can also be wonderful exercises for couples to do together.

TO ORDER

call **1–800–352–4037** or
Order direct from our website: www.onetribe.com

COMMUNE-A-KEY PUBLISHING AND SEMINARS

Commune-A-Key Publishing and Seminars was established in 1992. Our mission statement, "Communicating Keys to Growth and Empowerment," describes our effort to publish books that inspire and promote personal growth and wellness. Our books and products provide powerful ways to care for, discover and heal ourselves and others.

Our audience includes health care professionals and counselors, caregivers, men, women, people interested in Native American traditions—anyone interested in personal growth, psychology, recovery and inspiration. We hope you enjoy this book! If you have any comments, questions, or would like to be on our mailing list for future products and seminars, please write or call us at the address and phone number below.

ORDERING INFORMATION

Commune-A-Key Publishing has a variety of books and products. For further information on our books and audio tapes, or if you would like to receive a catalog, please write or call us at the address and phone number listed below. Our authors are also available for seminars, workshops and lectures. Please call our toll-free number for further information.

Commune-A-Key Publishing
P.O. Box 58637
Salt Lake City, UT 84158
•
1-800-983-0600

"This beautiful book touches that place within us that longs for a greater sense of community, and offers us practical ways to create that feeling of connectedness in our daily lives.

—Shakti Gawain, author of *Creative Visualization, Living in the Light,* and *The Path to Transformation*

"Call to Connection is an important book for our times. It does indeed, call us to connection. It reminds us how far we have strayed from our essential need for community and then gives us the keys we need to recreate it for ourselves, our families, and each other."

—Jack Canfield, co-author of *Chicken Soup for the Soul*

"A wonderful and imperative call to a way of life for reweaving the fabric of society. An authentic and ingeniously useful sacred work for healing our loneliness of heart and poverty of spirit. Listen and heed the call to connection so beautifully told by these modern day shamans. A simple, great book of true service that needs to be recognized... it belongs, even as we need to belong. Get it and follow it!"

—James Wanless, Ph.D., author of *Voyager Tarot: Way of the Great Oracle* and *Strategic Intuition for the 21st Century*

"Kammen and Gold are not only visionaries, they have forged simple yet practical tools for reclaiming the powers of nurturing and cooperation. They guide us through the mysteries of tribal living, with a prescription for healing the sense of separation and alienation so many of us are feeling in modern life."

—Hal Zina Bennett, Ph.D., best-selling author of *Follow Your Bliss,* and *Write From the Heart* and more than 25 published books on personal and spiritual development

"Call to Connection stirs one's soul. Its captivating accounts of ordinary people transforming their lives and practical "how to" exercises bring the benefits of tribe home to every reader."

—Richard Whiteley, author of winning best-sellers, *The Customer Driven Company* and *Customer-Centered Growth*